R00902 83826

```
LB          McPherson, Michael
2351.2        S.
.M34
1990        Selective admission
            and the public
            interest.        APR 0 2 1993

$10.95
```

| DATE | | | |
|---|---|---|---|
| | | | |
| | | | |
| | | | |
| | | | |
| | | | |
| | | | |
| | | | |
| | | | |
| | | | |
| | | | |
| | | | |
| | | | |

SOCIAL SCIENCES AND HISTORY DIVISION
THE CHICAGO PUBLIC LIBRARY

SOCIAL SCIENCES DIVISION
CHICAGO PUBLIC LIBRARY
400 SOUTH STATE STREET
CHICAGO, IL 60605

**BAKER & TAYLOR BOOKS**

# Selective Admission and the Public Interest

*Michael S. McPherson*

*and*

*Morton Owen Schapiro*

**Department of Economics
Williams College**

College Entrance Examination Board, New York

LB
2351.2
.M34
1990

The College Board is a nonprofit membership organization committed to maintaining academic standards and broadening access to higher education. Its more than 2,700 members include colleges and universities, secondary schools, university and school systems, and education associations and agencies. Representatives of the members elect the Board of Trustees and serve on committees and councils that advise the College Board on the guidance and placement, testing and assessment, and financial aid services it provides to students and educational institutions.

In all of its book publishing activities the College Board endeavors to present the works of authors who are well qualified to write with authority on the subject at hand and to present accurate and timely information. However, the opinions, interpretations, and conclusions of the authors are their own and do not necessarily represent those of the College Board; nothing contained herein should be assumed to represent an official position of the College Board or any of its members.

Copies of this book are available from your local bookseller or may be ordered from College Board Publications, Box 886, New York, New York 10101-0886 at $10.95.

Editorial inquiries concerning this book should be directed to Editorial Office, The College Board, 45 Columbus Avenue, New York, New York 10023-6992.

Copyright © 1990 by College Entrance Examination Board. All rights reserved. The College Board and acorn logo are registered trademarks of the College Entrance Examination Board.

Library of Congress Catalog Number: 90-084784

ISBN: 0-87447-399-3

Printed in the United States of America

# Contents

Foreword . . . . . . . . . . . . . . . . . . . . . . . . . . . . . . . . . . vii

Acknowledgements . . . . . . . . . . . . . . . . . . . . . . . . . . . ix

1. Introduction: Admissions, Equity, and
   Efficiency. . . . . . . . . . . . . . . . . . . . . . . . . . . . . . . . . . . 1

2. Who Goes to Which College?. . . . . . . . . . . . . . . . . 5

3. Values: The Range of Educational
   Outputs and the Concept of Justice . . . . . . . . . . . 13

   Educational Outputs . . . . . . . . . . . . . . . . . . . . . . . . . . . 14
      *Earnings Differentials* . . . . . . . . . . . . . . . . . . . . . . . . . 14
      *Academic Achievement* . . . . . . . . . . . . . . . . . . . . . . . . 16
      *Attitudes and Behavior* . . . . . . . . . . . . . . . . . . . . . . . . 18
      *Student Body Composition* . . . . . . . . . . . . . . . . . . . . . 22

Justice . . . . . . . . . . . . . . . . . . . . . . . . . . . 25
    *Theories of "Mutual Benefit"* . . . . . . . . . . . . . . . . 27
    *Institutional Autonomy* . . . . . . . . . . . . . . . . . . . 29

## 4. Models: How College Leads to Success . . . . . . . . . . . . . . . . . . . . . . . . . . 31

## 5. Trade-Offs: Must We Choose? What Are Our Choices? . . . . . . . . . . . . . . . . 35

Relevant Questions . . . . . . . . . . . . . . . . . . . . . . 35
Sorting Students by Ability . . . . . . . . . . . . . . . . . 37
Even Distribution of Students . . . . . . . . . . . . . . . . 38

## 6. Dilemmas: Competition and Coordination . . . . . . 43

Competitive Forces . . . . . . . . . . . . . . . . . . . . . . 44
Cooperative Agreements . . . . . . . . . . . . . . . . . . . . 47
    *Inequality-Preserving Agreements* . . . . . . . . . . . . . . 48
    *Inequality-Reducing Agreements* . . . . . . . . . . . . . . . 49
    *Results of Cooperative Agreements* . . . . . . . . . . . . . . 50
    *Coordination of Admission Policies* . . . . . . . . . . . . . 51

## 7. Policies: Big versus Small Changes . . . . . . . . . . . 53

A Radical Proposal: Pure Open Admission . . . . . . . . . . . 54
    *Advantages* . . . . . . . . . . . . . . . . . . . . . . . . . 55
    *Disadvantages* . . . . . . . . . . . . . . . . . . . . . . . 56
Intermediate Proposals: Modified Open Admissions . . . . . . . 57
Incremental Changes in the Existing System . . . . . . . . . . 59
    *Cooperative Agreements among Institutions* . . . . . . . . . . 59
    *Reallocation of Students* . . . . . . . . . . . . . . . . . . 61
    *Reallocation of Resources* . . . . . . . . . . . . . . . . . 63
Conclusions . . . . . . . . . . . . . . . . . . . . . . . . . 64

References . . . . . . . . . . . . . . . . . . . . . . . . . . 69

# Foreword

Each year, nearly one and a half million students across the country move directly from secondary school to the more than 3,000 colleges and universities in the nation. In addition, thousands of students enter higher education following a period of work or military service. This process whereby millions of young men and women annually choose, or are chosen by, colleges has been aptly described as "the great sorting."

In 1988, the College Board set out to conduct a comprehensive review of this great sorting—how students are distributed and distribute themselves across the variety of institutions of higher education in the United States—in an effort both to determine the extent to which the process serves the interests of students and institutions and, indeed, of the nation, and to demystify for parents and students the often-bewildering set of admission practices and procedures that mark the transition to college.

With the advice of professionals and experts in counseling, admission, financial aid, curriculum articulation, public policy, and professional associations, the *College Board Study of Admission to American Colleges and Universities in the 1990s* encompasses two series of monographs. The "Selective Admission Series," conceived by our colleague Fred A. Hargadon, Dean of Admission at Princeton Univer-

## Foreword

sity, and conducted under his leadership, addresses issues with particular implications for the more selective institutions (or, as Dean Hargadon has suggested, "institutions that engage in the process of selecting a class") and for the students who attend them. Recognizing that the majority of college-bound students attend a greater variety of institutions of higher education than those represented in the first group, the "Admission Practices Series" addresses additional issues of importance and concern to the educational community as a whole and the public at large. The two series are closely related and integral to the study.

During its history, the College Board has played an instrumental role in promoting consensus on ways to improve the efficiency, effectiveness, and fairness of the system of admission to college and the processes that surround that system. At a time when the means by which students find their way to particular institutions of higher education are marked with particular complexity, it is fitting that the College Board, as a unique membership association of schools and colleges, attempt to assess the degree to which the system as a whole serves the needs of the parties involved.

We owe special gratitude to the individuals who agreed to take on the task and the challenge of studying various aspects of the "great sorting" and, through these monographs, to describe the intricacies and strengths of our system of college admission.

*Donald M. Stewart*
President
The College Board

# Acknowledgements

We are grateful to Henry Bruton, Fred Hargadon, Peter Lipton, David Riesman, and Phil Smith for many helpful comments, but we absolve them of responsibility for the arguments we present. This study draws in part on data prepared with assistance from grants from the Andrew W. Mellon Foundation, the Spencer Foundation, and the Teagle Foundation. We appreciate their support.

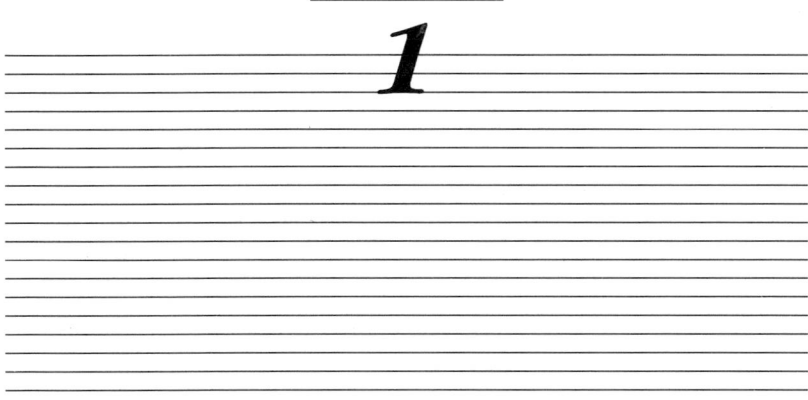

# Introduction: Admission, Equity, and Efficiency

This study describes how the American system of higher education distributes educational resources among students, and considers possible changes in that system. More precisely, we consider one distributive mechanism in the overall system: the practice of selective admission by a subset of all American colleges and universities.

It is odd to think of the United States as having a "system" for distributing higher education, for the distributive process is remarkably decentralized and uncoordinated. Selective admission, in particular, is the product of the uncoordinated (and sometimes slightly desperate) acts of individual institutions and individual students. Most of the actors in the game are, by necessity, focused on their fairly narrow sets of information and interests, guided only by a highly fragmentary picture of the whole.

Yet, from a broader perspective, there clearly is a whole: Selective admission, coupled with financial and other forces influencing students and institutions, yields a distinctive and reasonably systematic mechanism for distributing students across a range of postsecondary opportunities. B. Alden Thresher (1966) introduced a useful framework for viewing this system: Level one analysis is from the viewpoint of the individual student; level two is from the perspective of the individual college; and level three "presents a conspectus of the system as a whole, including the competitive and cooperative relationship among all the colleges in the matter of the entrance and exit of students" (p. 25). We propose here to try to view the admission process from the level three, or system, viewpoint and to ask some very basic questions: Does this mechanism for distributing students across schools serve the public interest? Could it be made to serve the public interest better? If so, how?

These are by no means simple questions. The values at stake are several and intertwined; the facts are complex; the forces at work are poorly understood. The main contribution of this monograph (as was true of Thresher's enlightening essay of over 20 years ago) lies, we think, in the shift of perspective from the individual student and institution to the system (or social) level. This shift in perspective raises more questions than it answers; they are, we think, good questions.

As one can quickly learn from an introductory text, economics is about trade-offs. The most fundamental of these trade-offs is between equity and efficiency; that is, a fairer or more equitable system often precludes a leaner, more productive one. At the same time, pursuing the goal of getting the most out of our resources may easily imply less attention toward what may be called "distributive justice."

Equity, or fairness, is itself a multidimensional concept. One aspect of it is a concern for the overall distribution of some sort of benefit: Does each economic class receive the proper share? A second aspect of equity is a concern for the fairness of the distributive processes: Is there discrimination against certain groups on irrelevant grounds? These two dimensions roughly correspond to "egalitarian" and "meritocratic" facets of equity, although, as we believe the later discussion shows, the two dimensions are harder to disentangle than that simple formulation may suggest.[1]

The trade-off between equity and efficiency is at the heart of many issues in higher education. Attempts to get the most out of our

---

1. One difficulty is that in fact we judge the fairness of processes partly by the outcomes they produce, and we judge the goodness of outcomes partly by the processes that produce them!

## Introduction: Admission, Equity, and Efficiency

educational system, whether results are measured in terms of its graduates' contribution to economic output, its faculty's contribution to scholarship, or in other ways, may be at odds with laudable aims of redressing various forms of disadvantage and providing an equitable distribution of resources across all segments of society.

However, such a trade-off need not apply in all cases. There may very well be ways to make changes in the way higher education operates in this country that make it not only more productive, but also fairer. At the very least, we should strive to minimize the adverse effect of one outcome on the other. Our goal in this monograph is to evaluate one aspect of our higher education system—selective admission—on the grounds of both equity and efficiency, with an eye to recognizing existing and potential trade-offs and seeking out policies that promote each goal without being too costly in terms of the other.

Of course, to pursue these issues, we must have a good idea of what both equity and efficiency actually mean and, if possible, some way of operationalizing each concept. Toward this end, particular attention will be paid to issues of measuring the equity and efficiency consequences of different admission policies.

The format of the monograph is as follows: Chapter 2 describes some main features of the outcome of the existing admission system in terms of the distribution of students across institutions. Chapters 3 and 4 analyze the consequences of higher education by enumerating and evaluating the various outputs of higher education in terms of what is "fair" and what is "efficient." Here, alternative descriptions of how the educational system actually operates are provided. Chapter 5 follows up the earlier work on defining and measuring equity and efficiency by turning to trade-offs between the two. Are they at odds in the current system? Must they be? Chapter 6 turns to a central issue underlying all of the discussion—the fact that individuals' (both students' and institutions') pursuit of their own goals may result in a collective situation in which achievement of those goals is frustrated. This dilemma is an important part of many economic analyses and seems central to an evaluation of our system of selective admission. Chapter 7 looks at what all of this means in terms of policy. Is there some fine tuning that would make our system operate better for all concerned? Alternatively, are things so bad that more substantial changes are called for?

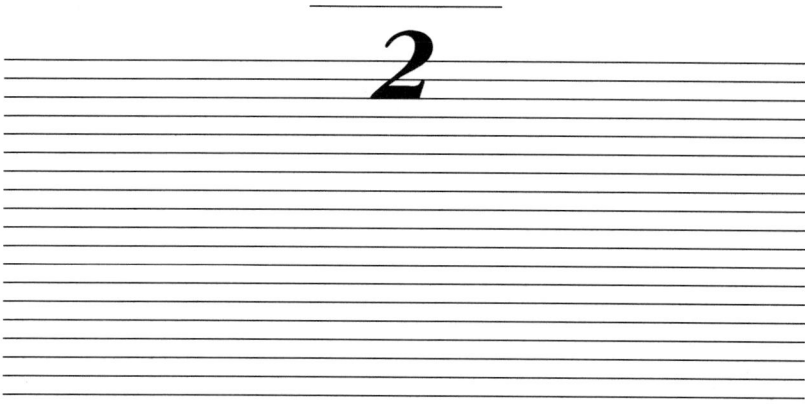

# Who Goes to Which College?

Before we begin our analysis of selective admission, we should examine how educational resources and opportunities are currently distributed. The variety of academic institutions in the United States is in many ways a unique strength. Colleges and universities differ in program offerings, residential settings, teaching methods, student body compositions, and many other factors. This variety makes it possible to accommodate an enormous diversity of student needs and preferences. The range of constituencies, sources of financial support, and modes of control help to preserve a multitude of values and perspectives and to ward off the specter of monolithic state control. And specialization of function allows particular institutions, such as the best of the research universities, to achieve levels of excellence that would be otherwise unattainable.

And yet the diversity of institutions also reflects and reinforces important social inequalities. There is an obvious broad correlation between resources spent per student and social background of students in American higher education. It is important not to exaggerate the differences in attendance patterns: There is a stronger representation of low-income and middle-income students in some types of private higher education than is sometimes realized. But important inequalities do exist, and although these result in some part from financial pressures, it is clear that the use of scholastic aptitude and academic achievement as screens for admission, in a society in which opportunity to acquire these aptitudes and attain these achievements is strongly influenced by family background, is a major factor.

The link between measured ability and family background deserves some further comment. The connection between economic status and Scholastic Aptitude Test (SAT) scores, for example, is quite apparent.[1] Hacker (1989) presented College Board data showing that the difference in SAT scores between low-income whites (family income of $10,000 to $20,000) and high-income whites (over $70,000) is 107 points (combined scores of 887 versus 994). The comparable economic status–SAT link for blacks and for Hispanics is even more striking (163 points and 162 points, respectively). These advantages are not limited only to test scores. Higher family income often provides better access to guidance counselors, more opportunities for international travel, a wider range of extracurricular activities, and other benefits that will make it more likely for students both to apply to, and to be accepted at, selective institutions. It should be noted that the decision about which schools to apply to is often critical to student destinations and can be heavily influenced by the quality of information and advice available to high school students.

A brief review of the relevant data provides a clearer picture of both the distribution of students across institutions and the resources spent per student at different types of institutions. Data from the fall of 1987 (College Board 1988) showed that the participation of whites in higher education ranges from a low at two-year institutions, where they make up 77 percent of enrollment, to a high at private liberal arts institutions, where they make up 90 percent of the student body. The picture for black students is reversed: They make up only 6 percent of the student body at private liberal arts institutions, while constituting 9 percent of the enrollment at two-year institutions.

---

1. This is not to say that test scores serve simply as a proxy for family income. At any income level, there is considerable variance in test scores. Presumably, the positive link between income and measured academic ability results from the educational and personal advantages that life in a higher-income family—and more affluent neighborhood—tend to bring.

Although minorities in general account for 19 percent of all students enrolled in institutions of higher education, they represent only 12 percent of the enrollment in private liberal arts institutions, but 20 percent of the enrollment in two-year institutions. Moreover, this difference is growing over time; from 1980 to 1987, minority representation in liberal arts institutions was constant, but it rose from 17.5 percent to 19.5 percent at two-year institutions.

These differences in types of institution attended are accompanied by differences in the percentages of students attending any college. Lee (1987), using High School and Beyond data collected by the National Center for Education Statistics, reported that in 1980, 54 percent of whites and 43 percent of blacks attended college in the first year out of high school. Thus, not only are whites more likely to attend college but, for those who do attend, their distribution across institutional types is quite different from that of students from other groups.

A breakdown by income, rather than race, finds similar results. Lee (1987) reported that the probability of going to college directly after high school is closely related to family income. Over two-thirds of students in his highest income group (over $38,000) attended college, but only about 38 percent of students in his lowest income group (under $7,000) did so. Astin et al. (1988) reported that students with family incomes above $60,000 per year are relatively rare (less than 18 percent of freshmen) at community colleges, but they represent slightly more than half of the enrollment at private universities.

Ability also plays a role in explaining persistence from secondary to higher education. Lee (1987) reported that only 28 percent of students in the lowest ability quartile went directly to college, but over 75 percent of those in the highest quartile did the same. In a breakdown combining income and ability, Hauptman and McLaughlin (1988) showed that enrollment rates for students with the highest skills but from the poorest families are about one-third less than the rates for students with equal ability but from the richest families (58 percent versus 86 percent). Similarly, students with the lowest skills but from the richest families are far more likely to attend college than are their poorer counterparts (40 percent versus 21 percent).

In sum, breakdowns by race, income, and ability all indicate that any goal of equal access for all students, at least if "equal access" is taken to imply similar results for similarly qualified individuals, is far from being realized in U.S. higher education. Moreover, differences in the allocation of resources across institutions imply very different educational experiences for different groups.

Lee (1987) examined differences in total educational subsidy across groups.[2] When students are broken down by income, the distribution of the subsidy tends to be equitable in the sense that students from higher income groups generally get smaller subsidies, but these differences are quite small. In 1983, students from the poorest families received an average total subsidy of $4,344, while students from the richest families received an average of $4,037. When the distribution of student aid (from all federal, state, and private sources) is considered, again the richest students receive less than the poorest students ($795 versus $1,262). Finally, the institutional subsidy (the difference between the amount institutions spend per student and the average tuition) can be examined. It is interesting to note that the institutional subsidy for the students from the poorest families is less than that for students from the richest families ($3,062 versus $3,187).

Replacing the income breakdown with a racial breakdown, Lee (1987) found that the total subsidy for blacks is greater than that for whites ($4,493 versus $3,839), reflecting a higher student aid subsidy ($1,188 versus $1,048) and a higher institutional subsidy ($3,278 versus $2,757). However, these differences are relatively small.

Turning to ability, Lee (1987) found that the total subsidy is positively related to relative ability; students in the lowest quartile receive an average of $3,225, and students in the highest quartile receive $4,836. Despite the fact that much of student aid is based on ability to pay, students in the highest ability quartile receive a much larger student aid subsidy than those in the bottom quartile ($1,468 versus $658). However, it should be kept in mind that higher ability students typically attend more expensive colleges, so that the gap between the "sticker price" and what parents can afford is greater.

---

2. The total subsidy is the amount of money from all sources provided for a student's education above and beyond individual or family contributions; this is the sum of education and general expenditures, grant aid, and grant-equivalent student aid, less the tuition paid by the student. For example, suppose a school with expenditures of $15,000 per student and tuition of $10,000 per student provides a student $1,000 in federally funded grant aid. That student then receives an institutional subsidy of $5,000 ($15,000 expenditure − $10,000 tuition) and a total educational subsidy of $6,000 ($5,000 institutional subsidy + $1,000 grant aid).

Finally, the institutional subsidy increases with ability, going from $2,562 for the lowest quartile to $3,327 for the highest.

In total, not only are high-ability students more likely than lower-ability students to attend college, but the subsidy they receive upon attending college is considerably greater than that received by their lower-ability counterparts. Although subsidies also vary with race and income, on the surface it appears that ability has the strongest effect. Of course, links among race, income, and ability complicate matters considerably.

A final point is that the type of institution attended affects the total subsidy received by a student. Although the average subsidy received by students attending private four-year institutions is only modestly above that received by students attending public four-year institutions ($5,605 versus $5,069), each is substantially above the subsidy received by students attending public two-year colleges ($2,394).

What all this means is that race, income, and ability matter in several ways. First, there are important differences in rates of progression between high school and college, according to where a student stands in terms of these three characteristics. Second, the type of institution of higher learning that is attended also varies across groups. If there were a fairly even allocation of resources across institutional types, these differences in enrollment across groups would not necessarily mean much. But resources are unevenly distributed, resulting in very different educational experiences and expenditures of social resources for different groups.

Plainly, not all of these differences in college-going outcomes are the product of college admission policies. Indeed, by some measures, very few American colleges and universities can be considered selective. If an institution accepting 75 percent or less of its applicants is considered selective, selective admission is fairly widespread. Extrapolating from available data (College Board 1988), in 1987, 48 percent of all four-year public institutions and 40 percent of all four-year private institutions fit into this category. On the other hand, if the criterion for selectivity were defined as accepting 50 percent or less of applicants, these percentages fall precipitously to only 10 percent and 9 percent, respectively. If all institutions of higher education are considered (there are over 1,300 two-year institutions in addition to approximately 1,800 four-year), the 50 percent criterion qualifies about 6 percent of the 3,100-plus institutions of higher learning in the United States as selective.

However, even if selective admission accounts for the placement of relatively few students, it has an obvious disproportionate effect on the placement of high-ability students. Moreover, there cannot be much doubt that selective admission has an important influence on the inequalities in student destinations described above. To be sure, low family income, even though its impact is partly offset by student aid, may push students toward less costly alternatives, such as community colleges, where levels of subsidy and the academic qualifications of students tend to be lower. Family background also influences student aspirations, so that patterns of student enrollment such as those described above are partly the result of differences in where students want to go to college, as well as which schools they are admitted to. Still, we know that there is a strong correlation between the selectivity of colleges, as measured by the ratio of their applicants to their admitted students, and their levels of per-student spending. It is also true that the wealthier institutions tend to be more selective, and that per-student spending at these institutions far exceeds that at less affluent schools.

McPherson, Schapiro, and Winston (1988, 1989b) presented data showing that educational and general (E&G) spending per student is almost 5 times higher at the private universities with the highest endowments per student (defined as more than $25,000—all endowments are as of 1979) than at the lowest-endowment private universities (less than $250 per student) and, strikingly, is over 13 times E&G spending per student at public two-year colleges.[3] At the highest-

---

3. The data set used to generate these numbers was constructed by merging two federally maintained data sets. One, the Financial Statistics report from the Higher Education General Information Survey, describes the basic financial accounts of all public and private nonprofit post-baccalaureate institutions in the United States, as well as a handful of "proprietary" trade schools that are run for profit. The second, the Fiscal Operations Report and Application to Participate data base, provides detailed information on student aid spending, revenues, and the population receiving aid at colleges and universities that apply for federal assistance under any of the so-called "campus-based" programs (direct loans, Supplemental Educational Opportunity Grants, and College Work-Study). We have merged data sets for all private nonprofit and public colleges and universities for the academic years 1978-79, 1983-84, and 1985-86. Data were drawn from data tapes created by the National Center for Education Statistics, supplied to the authors through the American Council on Education.

endowment private four-year colleges (more than $25,000 per student), E&G spending is almost three times that at the lowest-endowment private four-year colleges (less than $250 per student). For public universities, high-endowment institutions (more than $1,000 per student) spend more than twice as much per student as the lowest-endowment public universities (less than $250 per student), an amount that is six times the E&G spending at public two-year colleges.

Moreover, McPherson, Schapiro, and Winston (1989a) reported that although the gap in E&G spending per student has been narrowing between wealthier and less wealthy public institutions from 1979 to 1986, the opposite has occurred in the private sector. During that time period, E&G spending per student increased in real terms by 21 percent at the 148 private universities with endowments of less than $1,000 per student, while increasing 26 percent at the 79 private universities with endowments between $1,000 and $25,000 per student, and 22 percent at the 12 private universities with endowments of over $25,000 per student. Much more striking is the comparison among four-year private colleges; real E&G spending per student increased by 19 percent at the 371 colleges with endowments of less than $1,000 per student, 29 percent at the 151 colleges with endowments between $1,000 and $25,000 per student, and 35 percent at the 11 colleges with endowments of over $25,000 per student.

These numbers suggest that quality of education—at least so far as that is influenced by spending—varies widely across types of institutions. In addition, at private colleges and universities, the educational advantage held by students attending the richest, most prestigious institutions is growing over time. In sum, the amount of resources invested in a student depends critically on where the student goes to school.

The data reviewed in this chapter certainly do not "speak for themselves." We need to consider carefully the variety of evaluative issues raised by this information before drawing any policy conclusions about the role of selective admission in distributing higher education resources. Still, the facts about inequality in American higher education are compelling enough to urge us to take a hard look at these evaluative issues and at possible reforms in, or alternatives to, selective admission.

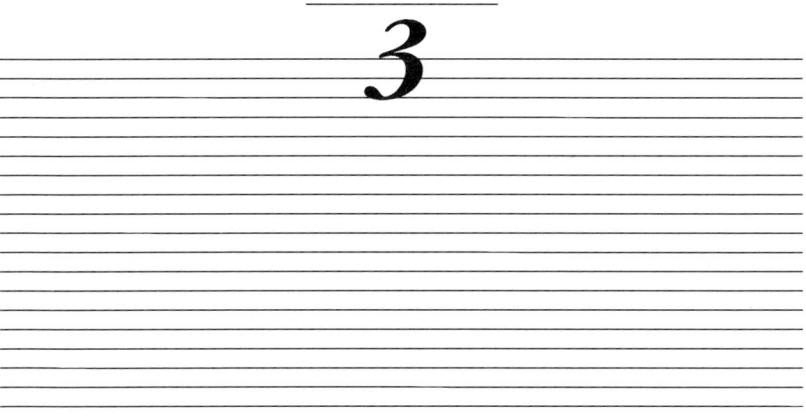

# Values: The Range of Educational Outputs and the Concept of Justice

Before we can meaningfully address issues of trading off efficiency and equity in higher education, we need to be clear on how each of these concepts applies in the special sphere of higher education.[1] It would be a mistake to construe efficiency narrowly, as concerned solely with the contributions higher education makes to economic growth or welfare. Rather, it is important to take a broad perspective on the kinds of valuable outcomes higher education provides or helps to promote. We also need a clear understanding of the various ways in which higher education contributes to improving people's lives before we can investigate the question of what it means to distribute the benefits of higher education equitably. Thus, we begin with a

---

1. A study that analyzes the recent history of higher education policy from the standpoint of the values of equity and quality is Hansen and Stampen (1987).

discussion of the various "outputs" of higher education before turning to issues of justice in the distribution of higher education.[2]

## Educational Outputs

Think about how we could describe—or, ideally, measure—the contributions of a particular college or university to the well-being of society. Some schools have significant effects through their research efforts or through service to their local communities, but for purposes of discussing selective admission, it makes sense to focus primarily on the impact of college on the lives of students. Certainly the most obvious "product" of a university or college is its graduates, and the key questions are: How does the college experience affect graduates' abilities and opportunities? How, in turn, do those factors affect society's well-being?

### *Earnings Differentials*

Perhaps the most obvious impact of college on students' lives (at least to an economist) is the earnings differential it permits them to command in the marketplace. A good deal of economic analysis has been premised on this view of the contribution of education to society. The assumption is that more education—what most economists call investment in human capital—eventually means higher levels of production in the workplace. There is extensive literature on this topic, devoted mainly to estimating the effect of additional years of schooling on the occupational destinations and earnings of workers. Many studies of earnings functions have sought to improve on this aggregate measure by replacing years of education with some measure of individual test scores.[3] The assumption is that the educational experience leads to greater cognitive skills, which translate into more

---

2. See McPherson (1983) and Schapiro (1988) for more detailed discussions of the various individual and social outcomes of higher education. The latter paper also considers how to use output measures in a productivity analysis.

3. These include Griliches and Mason (1972), Hause (1972), Hanushek (1973, 1978), Taubman and Wales (1974), and Hansen, Weisbrod, and Scanlon (1970).

productive workers, and that test scores are a better measure of these skills than the number of years of schooling.

However, there are problems in interpretation that accompany the analysis of the effects of education on wages, and these are not limited to the usual concerns about adequately controlling for background factors such as native ability. The finding that more years of education (or higher test scores) are correlated with higher earnings does not necessarily imply that education makes people more productive workers. Obviously, a link between wages and the value of a worker must be assumed and, even with this assumption, it is not clear whether the effect of education is actually to produce marketable skills.

An alternative hypothesis to explain why higher levels of educational attainment are usually correlated with higher wages is that the principal function of education is to screen for individuals with the greatest motivation and innate ability.[4] Plainly, distinguishing between more productive and less productive workers has some value, but not necessarily proportional to its costs. This is because a student who improves his or her position by passing through the educational "filter" will do so partly at the expense of others, who are thereby pushed back in the employment queue, so that the private return to the successful student exceeds the social return. The question of how college leads to success is an important one in any discussion of equity or efficiency; it is discussed further in Chapter 4.

A step beyond this concept of the value of education—that more years of education are linked to higher income—is to hypothesize a link between quality of education and eventual earnings. In the "human capital" version of this theory, more effective colleges add more to their students' cognitive capacities and hence to their economic productivity, thus producing higher eventual earnings. But a screening interpretation is also possible: What "good" schools (as conventionally defined) may do is to select, both for admission and for degree completion, students who have more capacity to be productive. If this is true, students will find it worthwhile to pay premium prices to attend "better" colleges, but the essential service the colleges perform is not to make the students more productive, but to *certify* their high productivity. As noted above, the private returns to students

---

4. See, for example, Spence (1973), Wolpin (1977), Riley (1979), and Weiss (1983).

from obtaining such certificates will, under plausible assumptions about how the economy works, exceed the social returns.

There is also some debate about the assumption that wage differences are a good measure of differences in the social contributions of different jobs. It is commonly acknowledged that certain careers (such as teaching, nursing, and legal aid) that deserve to be valued highly by society are nonetheless among the lowest paid. There is a more general question, discussed further below in the context of distributive justice, about whether the payments to the more highly paid occupations are genuinely necessary to gain the services of high-productivity workers.

## *Academic Achievement*

Wage gains are thus only an indirect and imperfect indicator of the economic contributions of education. Recently, there has been considerable interest in more direct measures of the effect of higher education on student learning, often relying on standardized tests. Good measures of the changes that actually occur in student capacities during college would be very helpful in understanding why college graduates earn more than others. Institutions interested in measuring how much their students have learned can contrast the results of standardized tests of their seniors with those of students from other institutions, but, of course, if the entrance standards differ, this comparison is meaningless. The best way to control for prematriculation quality is to test students early and use the results of these tests as a basis for comparison with later tests on the same students. This is what has been done, for example, at Northeast Missouri State University, an institution that has been at the leading edge of the assessment movement in this country. Even this sort of measure, of course, is unable to distinguish college effects from the simple effect of maturation on test performance.

**Standardized tests.** Some of these standardized tests are remarkably ambitious in the range of the educational accomplishments they aim to measure. The American College Testing Service (ACT), for example, has a broad-gauged evaluation tool called the College Outcomes Measures Program (COMP) Assessment that has been used by over 250 colleges and universities in the United States. The COMP assessment has three options: the composite exam, the objective test, and the activity inventory. The composite exam covers three "process" areas—oral and written communication, problem solving, and clarifying social values—and three "content" areas—functioning within social institutions, using science and technology, and using the arts. The objective test covers the same areas except that, unlike the composite exam, it contains no oral section and no essays. The activity inventory covers the same general areas as the other two exams but, unlike the others, is aimed at both current students and alumni, and seeks to determine what use the latter are making of their education. Other national organizations and a number of states are actively developing testing instruments that aim to assess the amount of learning accomplished in colleges.

However, some observers doubt whether any standardized exam can be used to measure accurately the output of education. John Chandler, former President of the Association of American Colleges, said:

> The use of standardized tests holds great promise for elevating minimum standards of student performance. But if standardized tests assume too prominent a role in an institution, they can have a stultifying effect on teaching and learning. Such tests are not well suited for permitting a student to demonstrate ... capacity for aesthetic judgement, critical thinking, moral sensibility, and other more subtle and elusive qualities of mind and character. (1986, pp. 7–8)[5]

This criticism is only one of several against an overconcentration on standardized exams. Another is the fear that faculty members will sacrifice substance in "teaching to the test." Not only is the authority of the instructor undermined by required standardized examinations, but these exams may encourage him or her to gear the course material to the norms of a general test, potentially sacrificing the risk-taking associated with the instructor's individual prerogative.[6]

**Other testing methods.** An alternative to standardized tests as a measure of the output of higher education is the use of either outside evaluators or panels of on-campus faculty members. A popular complaint about U.S. higher education is that teaching and the certification

---

5. See Boyer (1987) and Adelman (1986) for a similar argument, and Wigdor and Garner (1982) for a comprehensive discussion of issues in testing.

6. See Rentz (1979) for evidence that this has happened in states where institutional funding is tied to test results. On the other hand, Adelman (1986) argues that there is nothing necessarily wrong with teaching to the test.

plaint about U.S. higher education is that teaching and the certification of learning are usually "bundled," that is, done by the same individual.[7] The use of a senior comprehensive examination or paper through which students are evaluated by a panel of examiners would be a step in the direction of separating the teaching from the testing functions.

This is not exactly a novel idea. Swarthmore College, for example, has had an external examination system since 1922, under which faculty from other institutions not only grade a major written exam, but also give an oral examination.

The Association of American Colleges is conducting an experiment (funded by the Department of Education) in which participating colleges and universities are grouped by threes according to size, character, and region, and faculty examiners are exchanged among the schools (Chandler, 1986). For each school, a team consisting of faculty members from the other two schools in the group uses oral and written exams to assess how well seniors have been prepared in their major fields. The particular assessment tools, as well as the areas of coverage, are worked out in advance by the entire team. The purpose is to implement an assessment program that recognizes the value of a curriculum within the major that has some degree of uniformity across similar institutions but retains a role for individual autonomy of the faculty.

## *Attitudes and Behavior*

Is it possible to collect information on those aspects of educational output—leadership potential, moral integrity, and the ability to respond to new ideas and opportunities, for example—that cannot be measured on tests, from wage surveys, or from outside examiners? There are a number of survey instruments that seek to measure attitudes and behavior. These include 11 such surveys from ACT, 8 from Educational Testing Service (ETS), student outcome surveys from the National Center for Higher Education Management Systems, and value inventories that can be used to examine changes in student

---

7. See, for example, O'Neill (1983), Wang (1975), Harris (1972, 1986), Troutt (1979), and Chandler (1986). Boyer (1987) provides a historical perspective on this issue.

values during their academic careers.[8] Of course, to measure the effect of education, surveys should usually be completed early in the educational experience and again at a later point, although a meaningful comparison could be made between the results from alumni surveys from different institutions as long as their enrollment pools were similar (so that differences in outcome could be attributed to differences in schooling).

As we proceed in this way to broaden the range of educational outcomes we hope to assess, it is clear that the value of these outcomes extends beyond their contribution to the wage gains of individuals; leadership potential, responsiveness to new ideas, and so on, may plainly strengthen a person's performance as a citizen and in his or her personal life. Our present ability to measure such effects is even more doubtful than our ability to measure the relatively more straightforward wage effects, but that is no reason to neglect their potential importance. Although it is difficult to ascertain whether such social goals have been achieved, they include:

1. The enrichment of individual capacities for satisfying work, rewarding leisure, and self-development. The "quality" of individual lives becomes more important as material deprivations ease. If higher education can help us enrich both our leisure and our working lives, its contributions to individual well-being may be enormous.

Presumably college education can have such effects, partly by developing cognitive capacities that enrich the range of activities available to graduates, partly by providing a supportive environment in which emotional exploration and reflection can occur, and partly by exposing students to alternatives and possibilities they might not otherwise consider. All of these are features typically associated with liberal education.

2. Improved citizenship, enhanced political participation, and the development of community leaders. The tradition of democratic theory emphasizes the importance both of responsible and imaginative political leadership and of active and reflective citizenship. The latter may be thought to involve not only active political participation, but

---

8. See Harris (1986). Ewell (1983), Pace (1975, 1979, 1983, 1984), and McKenna (1983) discuss the formulation and analysis of student and alumni surveys.

also respect for the democratic virtues of tolerance, concern for justice, and the like, in everyday life.

3. The disinterested pursuit of truth (without regard to its economic value) in academic research.

4. The transmission, enrichment, and criticism of cultural traditions.

5. The provision of a secure forum for political and social criticism.

The last three functions, although distinct, are so interdependent that they warrant discussion together. Collectively, they represent a kind of social investment in the possibility of changing values. Academia plays (or is thought to play) the role of keeping open for examination the most cherished commitments a society has made. In principle, at least, commitment to these goals should ensure that no set of beliefs, whether about nature, society, or culture, becomes exempt from criticism. But, less obviously, such a commitment to critical reason is needed to make possible a fully meaningful affirmation of worthwhile values and beliefs; we cannot genuinely trust what cannot be examined and questioned. And by safeguarding traditions of critical inquiry in any of these areas—politics, natural science, the humanities—we help to safeguard them in the others, by underscoring that the fundamental standards and criteria in the academic realm are as independent as possible from the currently prevailing assumptions in society.

In addition to this list of noneconomic outcomes, one further output of higher education is said to have both economic and noneconomic consequences. T. W. Schultz, the dean of the human capital school, suggested insightfully that a key component in human capital is "the ability to deal with disequilibria"—to do something different when the occasion demands (Schultz, 1971, 1975). Education, according to Schultz, does not so much add to a person's capacity to do particular things as it strengthens his or her emotional and cognitive capacities to perceive and respond to change intelligently and resourcefully.

The lasting economic value of such education is especially apparent in a world where rapid technical changes make particular vocational skills quickly obsolete. But obviously education in this mode should also be well designed to meet the ends of liberal education: enhancing capacities for job satisfaction, productive leisure, and effective political involvement. Schultz, in fact, cited evidence that education, by improving the ability to deal with disequilibria,

## The Range of Educational Outputs and the Concept of Justice

increases nonmarket as well as market productivity. How fully the potential of this combination of liberal and vocational functions of education is actually achieved in practice is, of course, an important question to explore.

This discussion suggests a range of individual and aggregate output measures, some relatively easily quantified (such as wages), but somewhat ambiguously linked to schooling effects; others harder to measure (improved problem-solving ability), but more immediately connected to schooling. How should we define "efficiency" relative to such a range of outputs?

**Measuring efficiency.** Two important cautions must be registered as we examine the development of appropriate concepts in this area. First, it is important not to confuse improvements in indicators of output with improvements in the outputs themselves: Doubling the wages of college graduates by fiat would not be a social gain, whereas doubling the productivity of college graduates, with the result that their wages doubled, would be an increase in efficiency. Second, the large number of valued outcomes (and their partial incommensurability) must be recognized. Improving the economic productivity of college graduates at the expense of their capacity for self-expression or citizenship is an ambiguous gain. Only if we had a clear means of weighing these very different goods from a social point of view could we make a summary judgment. Otherwise, we may be forced to say merely that higher education is more efficient if it produces more of at least one valued output without producing less of any other (and without using more resources), or if the system uses fewer resources without producing less of any valued output. Notice that these problems may apply to the comparison of gains in education among different individuals, as well as among different kinds of educational output. How, for example, can we compare the educational gain from teaching elementary algebra to one student with the educational gain from teaching elementary calculus to another?

Of course, taken to extremes, these cautions could drive analysts of educational policy into silence. For some purposes, for example, it may be reasonable to weigh educational gains and losses accruing to different individuals according to the net economic value of the action; thus a distributional change that raises one person's wage by $10 per hour, at the cost of a reduction for another person of $5 per hour, should be judged an efficiency gain. In other cases, a measurement of cognitive achievement may be more suitable for efficiency comparisons. Suppose, for example, that resources could be redistributed in such a way as to reduce the scores of a group of 20 high achievers on some test from 650 to 600, while raising the scores of a group of 200 students from 500 to 550. Although we would surely want to know some details about the test before reaching a definitive judgment, it would be reasonable to contend that this change promoted educational efficiency.[9]

## *Student Body Composition*

How are educational outputs influenced by admission policies? Consider a set of simple hypothetical cases. Imagine two colleges with similar numbers of undergraduate students but very different positions in the universe of higher education. One institution, Schapiro College, is a highly selective institution with a strong endowment and high levels of spending per student. The other, McPherson Institute, is an unselective institution with very limited resources and low levels of spending per student. By most easily obtained measures, Schapiro College would be expected to provide a more "valuable" education than McPherson. Its students will have higher test scores, get better jobs, earn more money, and probably occupy positions where they will be able to make larger civic contributions.

Now suppose, in the first hypothetical case, that the student bodies of the two institutions are simply switched. What happens to "output"? By some conventional measures, the "quality" of McPherson will soar and that of Schapiro will plummet. Since the quality of the student body will be lower at Schapiro, in all likelihood the career destinations of its graduates will worsen and the seniors' performance on valuative tests will worsen. But this is obviously misleading. If the

---

9. The counterargument, of course, is that it might be worth reducing the scores of 1,000 students in order to increase those of a handful, if this would increase the odds of producing a Nobel laureate. This position might be justified on economic grounds, if we expect extraordinary gains from inventions the Nobelist might generate; on utilitarian grounds, if we argue that Nobelists have exceptional capacities for enjoying the "higher pleasures"; or on "perfectionist" grounds, if we argue that it is simply an intrinsically good thing to encourage the "higest" human achievements, even at the cost of more routine achievements for others. It might be noted that all these dimensions figured into Plato's and Aristotle's defenses of slavery.

final outcomes for the two groups of students are the same as before, we have no reason to say that the effectiveness of either institution has changed: each school simply has different "raw material" to work with.

However, given that Schapiro has a much richer endowment of resources, it is possible that the high-achieving students now going to McPherson will do less well than their predecessors at Schapiro did, and the lower achievers who were switched to Schapiro will do better than similar students who earlier attended McPherson. If this happens, it will provide evidence that schooling resources (or at least schooling reputations) really do affect educational outcomes.[10] Assuming that these are actual improvements in learning, rather than simply the effects of the institution's reputation, this indicates that moving students from a resource-poor to a resource-rich environment improves their educational achievement, and vice versa. However, it might still be hard to decide whether, on balance, the switch has raised or lowered the combined productivity of the two institutions. To decide this question would require balancing the gains for former McPherson students against the losses to former Schapiro students. This comparison raises distributive issues that we will return to below, but some comparisons might meaningfully be made on a pure efficiency basis. How do test-score gains for the low achievers, for example, compare to drops in test scores for the high achievers? Do wage gains for the low achievers exceed the losses for the high achievers?

A variant on this hypothetical case adds a dimension to it. It is possible that both institutions were particularly suited to their particular clienteles before the switch. (Indeed, it is conceivable that the resources at Schapiro are so tailored to the education of high achievers that the low achievers do worse by being transferred there.) Suppose that after the switch, relative per-student spending is kept at its previous level at each institution, but each is permitted to revise its staffing and curriculum to make them more appropriate for the new student populations. Such adjustments would presumably make each institution more productive than it would have been in the first

---

10. If the gains to students moving to Schapiro are the result only of the institution's better reputation, we would expect them to disappear over time, as the reputation of the institution adjusted to its new student body composition.

hypothetical case. Thus, we isolate the impact of differences in resources per student on the educational effectiveness of more and less selective institutions. Compared to the first case, we expect bigger gains for the low achievers and smaller losses for the high achievers than in the original experiment.

Consider one further variation. Students learn from one another, and in the original scenarios, the students bring all their peers with them in moving from one institution to another. (Each student in the high-achieving group also benefits from any "halo" effect resulting from being grouped with these high achievers.) Suppose instead that only half the students from each institution are switched. We can now ask how the outcomes for the students switched in this case compare to those in which all the students are switched. We can also ask about the impact of the switch on the students who stay put. It is clear that several issues are raised: Do the teachers at a school work more effectively when they have homogeneous or heterogeneous groupings of students? How is the performance of lower-achieving students influenced by being educated in the presence of higher-achieving students? How is the performance of higher-achieving students influenced by being educated in the presence of lower-achieving students?

We do not have much empirical evidence to answer these questions, but one plausible outcome is that the low-achieving students moved to Schapiro do somewhat better under this experiment than under the earlier scenarios, and that the low achievers who stay at McPherson likewise do better than they did when only low achievers were at McPherson. This suggests (consistently with some inconclusive evidence to be examined in Chapter 5) that high-achieving students contribute to the education of their lower-achieving peers. What is the likely outcome for the high achievers? If they had benefited previously from the presence of high-achieving colleagues, it is likely that their performance will worsen at both institutions, compared to what it is when all the high achievers are grouped together. This raises again the issue of how to balance the gains to one group against the losses to another. A more detailed look at these trade-offs and the empirical literature that attempts to understand them is contained in Chapter 5.

These simple hypothetical cases underline the complexity of making judgments about the educational impact of changes in admission practices. It is necessary to determine the effect of admission policies on the value added by a school, rather than simply on the quality of the students that the school attracts. In considering value added, we must expect that the level of resources a school has available, the degree to which those resources are specially adapted to students with different aptitudes, and the nature of peer effects will all be important variables. These issues bear not only on the efficiency effects of admission policies but also on their equity effects, which we consider in the following section.

## Justice

The broad facts about the distribution of higher education by income and ability reviewed in Chapter 2 raise a fundamental issue about the fairness of these arrangements. The basic fact is that those who start in life with the natural advantage of greater "innate" talents (as talents are measured and rewarded in our society) and/or with the social advantage of being born in circumstances that provide greater access to high-quality elementary and secondary education and a more educationally supportive home environment receive more and better education at the postsecondary level. In fact, not only does this privileged group "consume" more educational resources in college, but it also has larger amounts spent on its education by society, through government and institutional subsidies. The system seems to pile advantage on advantage, reinforcing initial inequalities through unequal distribution of educational resources, which seems unfair.

The most obvious justification for providing more and better education to the more able appeals to the value of efficiency. More able people, we might say, can benefit more from access to educational resources, and thereby contribute more to society through their use, than others. Everybody benefits from investing more heavily in the education of those with more academic potential. This argument has obvious force, but it raises at least three issues that call for more careful attention.

First, there can be too much of a good thing. It is quite likely that, starting from a position of complete equality in the distribution of education among more and less able students, there would be efficiency gains from increasing spending on the more able at the expense of spending on the less able. But the benefits of such resource shifting may be subject to diminishing returns, whereby at some point so much shifting of resources toward the more able has taken place that further shifting will actually harm efficiency.[11] Where that point is, and whether we are beyond it, is not something we know much about empirically, although an intriguing study of this question by Daniere and Mechling (1970) is discussed in Chapter 5.

Second, the inequalities in ability among students at the end of high school are in substantial measure the product of earlier social inequalities, which may themselves be unfair. Thus, one way of defending inequalities in the distribution of higher education resources is in terms of the value of equal opportunity: Competitive admission processes (at least when coupled with ability-to-pay financing) provide everybody with an equal chance at getting into one of the favored positions. But equalizing opportunities at the end of high school has a somewhat hollow ring; such factors as where you went to high school, what your neighborhood was like, and how much part-time work you had to do produce very considerable inequalities of opportunity to develop the capacities that govern admission to "good" colleges. A significant moral dilemma for higher education policy is raised by the persistence of these deep-rooted inequalities in opportunity. For if these class-based inequalities in life chances did not exist—if, by the end of high school, students had had genuinely equal opportunities to develop their capacities—the potential conflict between the values of efficiency and of equal opportunity in distributing college education would be greatly reduced. We could be confident that those young people who failed to show academic promise had had a fair chance, and we could be more comfortable in devoting resources to the more promising students (if that is what efficiency recommended). As things stand, though, college may represent an important "second chance" for those whom the system has failed. The ideal (utopian?) solution is to fix the underlying inequalities so that such second chances are not needed; failing that, it is difficult to say how far the distribution of higher education resources should help promote more equal opportunity by compensating for the effects of inequalities in earlier life.

Third, the idea that everybody benefits from unequal educational investments depends crucially on how the social benefits from these investments are shared. This focuses attention on how society rewards educational attainments. If those who get the "best" educations qualify for important jobs with large financial rewards and great social pres-

---

11. See Chapter 5 for an explanation of this hypothesis.

tige, it may still be true that everybody benefits from these educational investments if the alternative is that those jobs go unfilled or are filled by less well educated people, but the benefits would be more equitably shared if the same people filled those jobs while receiving more modest salaries.

## *Theories of "Mutual Benefit"*

Recent philosophical writing has sharpened reflection about the meaning of this concept of mutual benefit. John Rawls (1971) has suggested that we should define "mutual benefit" in reference to a baseline of complete equality: Social institutions (including higher education) should not be allowed to benefit the better off at the expense of harming those who are worse off. Inequalities, then, are justified if their ultimate result is to benefit the least well off in society. So we could say that higher incomes for Harvard graduates are justified if they are needed to attract good students to Harvard and then to the jobs such students fill. But those inequalities should be the smallest that will get the job done. Alternatively, we could define mutual benefit by a standard not of equality, but of the best everyone could do under conditions of complete social noncooperation (a "state of nature"). According to this theory, advocated by Robert Nozick (1974) and David Gauthier (1986), inequalities harm a group only if they deprive it of the minimal living conditions it could eke out in isolation. This is obviously a much weaker standard than Rawls's.

These two theories represent widely disparate views. Rawls urges the maximum equality that is consistent with efficiency; Nozick and Gauthier provide a minimal commitment to equality. One natural, and perhaps justified, response to these polar views is to search for a plausible middle ground: a baseline more demanding than the state of nature but less demanding than complete equality. It is also, however, illuminating to probe a little further into the concepts of justice that underlie the two more extreme positions. For Rawls, a governing insight is the view that the natural and social advantages some people possess are "arbitrary from a moral point of view" (Rawls, 1971). The gifts and talents possessed by members of the community are best viewed as a collective asset, which can and should be used to better everyone's condition, in circumstances that protect everyone's basic liberties and autonomy. Rawls's belief that we cannot be said to *deserve* our natural or social advantages leads to the view that distributive institutions should, first, ensure equality of opportunity so far as possible and, second, share the benefits of remaining inequalities in natural assets as broadly as possible.

The resulting dismissal of merit or "natural entitlement" as independent bases for distribution has been seen by many critics, including Nozick, as disturbing. Although it is conceded that people cannot be said to "deserve" talents and capacities they were born with, it does not necessarily follow that they therefore cannot claim to deserve, or be entitled to, any of the fruits of their talents. Perhaps a soldier does not deserve the accidents of background and circumstance that lead him to perform an act of heroism, but that does not mean that he does not deserve a medal; we do not, as Nozick says, have to deserve things "all the way down." In effect, Nozick's theory minimizes the constraints on entitlements imposed by principles of equality, thereby maximizing the latitude permitted for differences in individual entitlement. This results in a theoretical view that would, for example, unblinkingly accept indefinitely large deviations in the educational opportunities of children born in different circumstances.

There is, however, a different (and, to us, more congenial) way to permit some consideration of merit or entitlement in determining educational distribution. Notice that for Rawls, with his view of talents as collective assets to be shared, the only reason to provide more or better education for the more talented is efficiency—this allocation may do more for the collective social good. Suppose, however, that we distinguish two aspects of the distributive consequences of educational policies: (1) intrinsic benefits of education, and (2) the external social rewards of educational achievements. Intuitively, it seems that those with exceptional academic talent deserve the chance to develop that talent as far as possible (except in a society where highly urgent social needs were not being met). Indeed, rewarding academic merit in this way can be seen as embodying a conception of "equity." Certainly the argument that education should go to the most academically qualified students has been an important argument against distributing education on the basis of social privilege. It remains troubling, however, that in our society, education, even when allocated according to academic potential, quite often yields large extrinsic rewards in material benefits or social prestige. Academically gifted people seem (often) to get a double benefit: not only the enjoyment of their talent and the chance to fulfill it, but access to unusually well-rewarded material lives as well.

Imagine a society where the material rewards for academic achievement were substantially less than now—which would surely be true of a society where educational opportunity was more widely distributed. (In our society the scarcity of academic talent derives in good part from the fact that much potential talent is never developed.) If we could reduce the correlation between access to a high-quality education and access to a materially successful life, we might be considerably less bothered by the idea that those with more academic talent deserve to receive more and better educational resources. Michael Walzer expressed this viewpoint nicely:

> Schools cannot avoid differentiating among their students, advancing some and turning others away; but the differences they discover and enforce should be intrinsic to the work, not to the status of the work. They should have to do with achievement, not with the economic and political rewards of achievement; they should be inwardly focused, matters of praise and pride within the schools and then within the profession, but of uncertain standing in the larger world.... I am describing not schools for saints but only centers of learning rather more insulated than at present from the business of "making it." (1983, p. 211)

## *Institutional Autonomy*

The value of the autonomy of educational institutions is distinct from the values of efficiency in educational production and distributive justice toward individuals. The principle that educational institutions should have substantial freedom from political control over their operations is deeply connected to traditions of academic freedom and to our understanding of the role of colleges and universities in our society. As Supreme Court Justice Felix Frankfurter put it in a celebrated decision, " 'the four essential freedoms of the university' [are] to determine for itself who may teach, what may be taught, how it shall be taught, and who may be admitted to study."[12] As long as universities are granted the right to choose whom to admit, there is a substantial likelihood that the wealthier and more prestigious universities will elect to admit the more able students. There may not

---

12. *Sweezy* v. *New Hampshire,* 354 U.S. 234 (June 17, 1957) at 263.

be any means compatible with respecting academic freedom that would prevent these inequalities from occurring.

These considerations operate as an important constraint on the kinds of policies governments can properly follow in influencing the admission policies of universities and colleges. Even if there were widespread social agreement on desirable changes in the distribution of students among institutions, there would be no permissible way for the federal government to dictate that result (or for states with substantial numbers of independent institutions to do so). Regarding state-run institutions, presumably governments have considerably wider discretion, constrained by principles of fairness and nondiscrimination.

This limitation does not, however, render the discussion of the public interest in selective admission pointless. First, level three thinking, described in Chapter 1, may still have a place in the deliberative processes of individual institutions. Second, institutions may choose to cooperate in some aspects of their admission policies, and the principles underlying cooperative agreements may partly reflect concern for the public interest. (We return to this point in Chapter 6.) Last but not least, government policies toward higher-education institutions may create substantial incentives for those institutions to revise their admission policies. There will always be the question of whether such attempts to manipulate the behavior of institutions become unacceptably intrusive in the internal affairs of institutions. But there seems to be considerable scope for encouraging cooperative behavior among institutions, and using government policies toward institutions in legitimate ways to encourage socially desirable behavior concerning admission. This is discussed in Chapter 7.

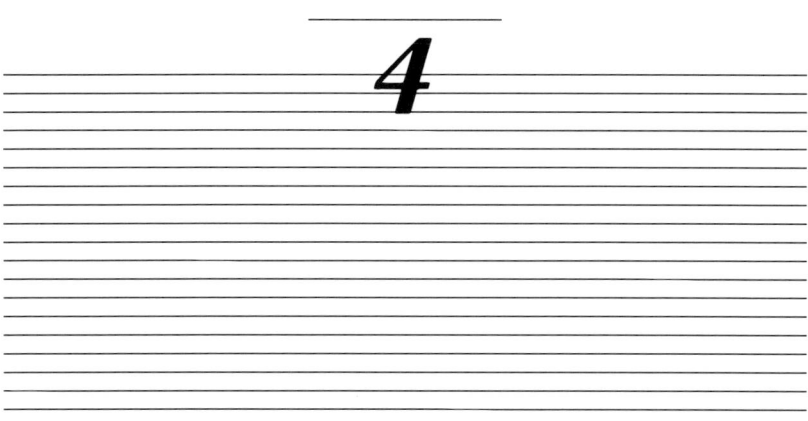

# Models: How College Leads to Success

Empirical studies in the human capital tradition (Griliches and Mason 1972; Hause 1972; Hanushek 1973, 1978; Taubman and Wales 1974; Hansen, Weisbrod, and Scanlon 1970) assume that education raises people's incomes by making them more productive, though typically they say little about what it is about education that has this effect—college is a "black box" from which people emerge more productive than before. Presumably, education works either by supplying people with specific vocational skills or by improving their more general cognitive and affective capacities in productivity-enhancing ways.

A contrasting view has been labeled the screening hypothesis: Education works to raise an individual's income not by changing the person at all, but simply by identifying and certifying talents he or she already had, thereby making those preexisting capacities more marketable (Spence 1973; Wolpin 1977; Riley 1979; Weiss 1983). To the extent that higher education fills such a "credentialing" function, it simply presents itself to the student as a set of hurdles, arbitrary from the standpoint of adding to the student's skills or knowledge, that must be negotiated on the way to a career. This perception is likely to be highly destructive to the social and political attitudes higher education is supposed to promote. In Thurow's apt phrase (1975, p. 96), higher education will seem a "defensive necessity," engaged in not for its positive value, but to avert the disastrous career prospects awaiting those without the right credentials. Students see themselves running farther and faster to get to the same place in the hierarchy that their parents occupied.

A third, more radical view, associated especially with Bowles and Gintis (1976), is that education does indeed change people, but not principally or most relevantly in cognitive ways. Rather, education adapts people to specific roles in a class-divided society; in particular, it socializes people into roles as "bosses" and "workers."

These contrasting theories obviously have very different implications for the social significance of education's economic contributions. In the human capital version, education adds straightforwardly to the nation's wealth. Because education makes persons more productive, the returns they receive from education reflect the greater output they provide. If this is correct, education (both precollege and higher), is a major contributor to economic growth. But if education mainly screens or filters people, its contributions to economic efficiency are less clear. Plainly, sorting out more productive and less productive workers is worth something, but not necessarily as much as it costs. This is because when one student improves his or her position by passing through the educational "filter," the student will be doing so partly at the expense of others who are thereby pushed back in the employment queue, so that the return to the individual student is greater than the social return, taking into account the losses of others. Extending educational "ladders"—requiring a college degree for a job that used to require only a high school diploma—may not improve the sorting process very much, and adds considerably to private and social costs. These external losses do not emerge under the human capital view.

The screening hypothesis thus suggests that educational investment may be economically dysfunctional or pointless at the margin. Interestingly, the radical view makes a different claim: Educational investment is highly functional within the context of capitalism, for it not only sorts people among roles, but develops in them the noncognitive traits that these roles demand. Thus the radical can concede that education has been vital for past economic growth and, further, that educational socialization in some form would be needed in any society. However, the radical claims that the specific roles themselves are dysfunctional: Educational socialization for capitalism is limiting and alienating, when, in a society with a different social structure, it could be liberating.

The choice among these views is remarkably resistant to empirical resolution, in part, no doubt, because each contains some truth as a description of American higher education. Surely, as human capital theory claims, some forms of higher education develop in people cognitive traits of real social and economic value; as advocates of the screening hypothesis contend, education serves in part to test for and to certify preexisting traits; and finally, as the radicals claim, some aspects of higher education serve more to reconcile people to their place in existing social arrangements than to foster their own development.

It is entirely possible that the degree of stratification in American higher education is greater than can be justified from any of these three viewpoints. Plainly, the radicals would regard a highly stratified system as incompatible with favorable human development. Advocates of the human capital approach would want to know whether such a high degree of stratification maximizes the production of human capital. Proponents of the credentialing viewpoint would be concerned that highly stratified educational arrangements would lead to overinvestment in obtaining credentials. It thus seems worthwhile from all viewpoints to investigate policies that might reduce admission stratification. We consider such policies in Chapters 6 and 7.

# Trade-Offs: Must We Choose? What Are Our Choices?

How should the need to develop fully the talents of the most able students be weighed against the claims of less able or disadvantaged students for assistance? Although more able students, as measured by grades and SAT scores, plainly get more and better education in this society than do less able students (recall the discussion in Chapter 2), many believe that not enough is done (particularly at the elementary and secondary levels) to develop the talents of the most gifted. However, an opposing viewpoint is that the less able should receive at least as much attention as the more able, especially because lower measured ability is very often a consequence of a deprived family and community environment.

## Relevant Questions

**How great is the need for the talents of the most able?** Extra expenditures on the most able, and generous rewards to motivate their efforts, may even be justified from the viewpoint of the other students, if the contributions of the most able to a workable modern society are essential and can be obtained in no other way. But, at the same time, it may be true in our society that candidacy for the intellectual elite is influenced by inequalities of social background that affect measured ability, and the apparent scarcity of talent may be partly a function of those inequalities. Thus, there may be a difficult conflict between exploiting available talent in the short run and fostering reduced inequalities (and expanded talent pools) in the long run.

**How much value is "added" to students at differing ability levels by investment in their education?** Although intellectual talent is valuable, it may be argued that, at the margin, increased expenditures on those with a great deal of talent may bring a smaller return than increased expenditures on those with less, especially considering that expenditures are already much higher for the more able. The high quality of the product of elite institutions may, it is argued, reflect the high quality of the students they attract, rather than how the institutions mold the students. If this is the case, efficiency and equality may not conflict, as is so often alleged; more able students would excel even if fewer resources were devoted to their education. An important issue in this context is whether we know how to spend education dollars effectively on low-achieving students at the college level.

**What are the educational implications of alternative student allocation schemes?** Is there an empirical justification for sorting students by ability, or will we be better served by a more even distribution of students by ability across all types of institutions?

**How much responsibility should higher education bear for addressing the needs of the disadvantaged?** The roots of the disabilities of students may lie in failings of other social institutions: poor distribution of income, weaknesses in elementary/secondary education, and proliferation of ghettos and slums. Granted that disadvantaged youth deserve much more than they get from society, there is considerable disagreement about whether the best strategy for such spending is to attempt to repair earlier damage so late in the game, rather than helping these groups in other, and perhaps more basic, ways. Perhaps the hardest question is what to do if this other help is not forthcoming: When other institutions continue to fail these youth, should higher education try to pick up the pieces?

# Sorting Students by Ability

An important issue in the evaluation of alternative allocation schemes is the effect of sorting students according to ability. Selective admission is obviously a sorting mechanism in which students with the highest abilities are grouped together, leaving lower-ability students in a separate group. Does this sorting mechanism have the undesirable effect of selecting according to racial and socioeconomic group as well as ability? Does the particular track a student is placed in have a strong effect on the educational experience that student encounters? What would happen if students were more evenly distributed by ability across a range of institutions?

Although there is surprisingly little known about the effects of alternative allocation mechanisms at the higher education level, there has been a good deal of work done at the secondary school level, where, according to the National Education Association (1968), about 90 percent of all high schools use some form of sorting. However, even there, a consensus has not emerged about the effects of this practice.

Vanfossen, Jones, and Spade (1987) summarized this literature, reporting that some studies found curriculum tracking or sorting operates to allocate students according to their different backgrounds and leads to very different educational experiences, thereby facilitating the transmission of class status from one generation to the next; other studies also cited in Vanfossen et al. found that the sorting is done primarily according to ability rather than class background, thereby facilitating social mobility; and still others found that sorting by whatever criteria makes little difference in ultimate educational outcome.

The study by Vanfossen, Jones, and Spade used data from the High School and Beyond data set and found that tracking sorts students according to both socioeconomic background and ability, and that track location is in fact a fairly important determinant of a variety of educational outcomes including academic performance, educational aspirations, and the like.

These authors concluded that although many school officials maintain that learning is aided by grouping together students with similar abilities, they neglect the role that socioeconomic status plays in determining the track a student is placed in. (For example, a very good student from a disadvantaged socioeconomic group has a substantially lower probability of being placed in an academic track than a more affluent counterpart of similar ability.) The particular track not only affects secondary school, but extends into postsecondary education.

But why do students on a lower track end up suffering academically? The authors speculated that teachers may treat these students differently and, in addition, following Coleman et al. (1966), that a critical mass of interested and enthusiastic students is needed in order to push along the learning process. Also, the best teachers may be attracted by the opportunity to teach the best students and, hence, teacher quality may vary positively with student quality.

If these findings carry over to college, an admission scheme that sorts students, as our selective admission system currently does, is likely to sort according to socioeconomic status, partly because of the correlation between socioeconomic status and ability. Further, the educational experience of an average student at an institution that attracts less than stellar students is likely to be inferior to that at an institution where there are a larger number of better students. The facts described in Chapter 2 support these hypotheses; students from lower socioeconomic backgrounds more often attend institutions that have a relatively large number of similar students, and the amount of resources allocated to the students' education is relatively small. Students from a more affluent background more often attend institutions with other affluent students and benefit from a relatively generous allocation of resources.

## Even Distribution of Students

Thresher (1966) stated that there are two issues relating to the "great sorting" of students among colleges. One is determining what is actually happening. "But if the ultimate object is to study not merely college admissions as a system, but 'college admissions and the public interest,' there is the much more difficult problem of trying to decide what the sorting *ought* to be" (p. 83).

An alternative allocation scheme would be to group students in a more random fashion—in other words, to stream. Taking better students away from institutions in which they predominate and putting them in lower quality institutions may improve the educational experiences for all students at these less prestigious institutions if this motivates both teachers and other students to be more engaged in the learning process. If resources were allocated in a similar manner—taking some from the "better" schools and giving more to the "worse" (poorer) schools—the positive effect of this reallocation of students would probably be increased. The study described in the following paragraph recommends just such a change.

Daniere and Mechling (1970) computed expected earnings flows for students with different abilities entering institutions of differing quality. When benefit-cost ratios are examined, the conclusion is reached that we have gone too far in an allocation scheme that places high-aptitude students in high-quality institutions and low-aptitude students in low-quality institutions. Instead, these authors recommended that we pursue a policy in which additional college places should go to higher-aptitude students who attend low-cost and low-quality institutions.

Although this striking conclusion is sensitive to a number of assumptions, one of which is that the sole educational output is the increase in national output, it nonetheless encourages the consideration of alternative allocation schemes, at least on efficiency grounds. It certainly lends credence to Thresher's (1966) comment that "It has not by any means been demonstrated that the overall welfare of the nation or of humanity would best be served by concentrating all the ablest students in a few of the strongest universities" (pp. 22–23). He said further that although some floor is needed in terms of preparation and aptitude,

> above this floor, a good argument can be made for something like a random choice of applicants. Then each college will be more nearly carrying its fair share of the load of providing education. It will in time come to be judged by the "value-added" to its alumni, and it will have the satisfaction of knowing that its achievement is inherent and earned, not adventitiously and artificially gained through shunting a super-select group into its gates. (p. 58)

This proposal is examined in detail in Chapter 7. But such a scheme would plainly bring some losses to accompany the gains. The interests of some students and, quite possibly, the efficiency effects of the higher education system would be enhanced, but some students would be hurt.

An interesting paper by Henderson, Meiszkowski, and Sauvageau (1978) described these differential effects in detail. Looking at primary school data from Canada, they found that there is a strong peer group effect: The achievement of individual students depends to a large extent on the quality of their classmates. The efficiency gain from streaming comes from the nonlinearity of this effect: The achievement of individual students rises with an improvement in the average quality of their classmates, but the increment in achievement falls as average class quality rises. That is, removing a superior student from a class composed of other superior students and placing him or her in a class of weak students will raise the achievement level of the weak students more than it will reduce the achievement level of the class that the student left. Hence, mixing weak and strong students raises the overall performance of the student population, as the gains of the weak students exceed the losses of the strong students.

Although this finding is quite controversial, it suggests that efficiency gains come at the expense of some individuals who are hurt while others are helped. This trade-off, although quite common in economics, forces us to make difficult decisions regarding relative weights for winners and losers.

In a provocative article, Karabel (1972) reviewed evidence on the academic performance of able students at a variety of types of institutions and concluded:

> This evidence, though by no means definitive, does indicate that a gifted student at an unselective institution does not mysteriously lose his talents.... the success of the academically able in almost any institutional setting should not be too surprising; the bright have a capacity for taking care of their own education. (p. 35)

However, others argue that a more random distribution of students across institutions would lead to substantial efficiency costs, as represented by the view of Reder (1974):

> Clearly, it is inegalitarian—elitist—for universities to foster the conferring of lifetime socioeconomic advantage upon individuals possessing characteristics (e.g., academic capacity) best acquired in a middle- or upper-class environment. Yet it is extremely difficult for a university to remedy the matter. Whether it is possible, through

> later education, to offset the adverse effect on academic performance of cultural deprivation in the early years of life (before age 15) is not clear. What is clear is that, at present, no one has the necessary know-how. In consequence, if universities are to include larger percentages of lower-status youths than heretofore—especially from racial and cultural minorities—they must increase the relative weight attached to promoting socioeconomic equality, and decrease that placed upon intellectual achievement. (p. 425)

Although Reder gives no empirical evidence supporting his position, it should be pointed out that no definitive evidence either refuting or confirming this view has yet been provided by researchers.

One possible reason for such a negative educational result of streaming is increased difficulty for teachers in coping with a wider range of talents and interests within the classroom. Clearly, it can be hard to keep the brightest students interested without losing the interest and comprehension of those who are less capable. At the same time, if the range of abilities in a class is handled creatively, it may be used to educational advantage—for example, by getting the more advanced students to help educate the others. Again, we know little empirically about how to weigh the educational drawbacks and advantages of streaming.

Assume that subsequent research convinces us that the efficiency of higher education, in terms of the overall achievement level of its students, could be increased by eliminating selective admission and moving to a system like that described by Thresher (1966), but that some students will lose. How do we weigh the losses borne by stronger students against the gains garnered by weaker students?

One reason that such a system could be justified on equity grounds is that the association between student ability and socioeconomic background implies that the students who are gaining are from relatively disadvantaged backgrounds, and those who are losing are not. Hence, this kind of allocation scheme can be thought of as leveling the playing field; more affluent students, who have had more resources invested in them before college, then augment the educational experience of students who have had fewer resources invested in them before college. Of course, an enrollment scheme that sends many more high-ability students to relatively low-quality institutions should probably be accompanied by the allocation of government funds in a more equitable way, so that these students have access to enough resources to ensure their own development and the development of their classmates. Even if this were done, postsecondary educational experiences for more affluent/higher ability students might still be worse under streaming than under sorting, but this might be a fair price to pay, given the redistributive effects of such a plan. Other effects of this sort of scheme, including possible motivational impacts on high school students, are discussed in Chapter 6.

The evidence is only scattered, but it is possible that our existing system of selective admission fails on both efficiency and equity grounds—that a more random allocation scheme may make the system both more efficient and fairer. We return to this point in Chapter 7, where we suggest possible changes in the current system.

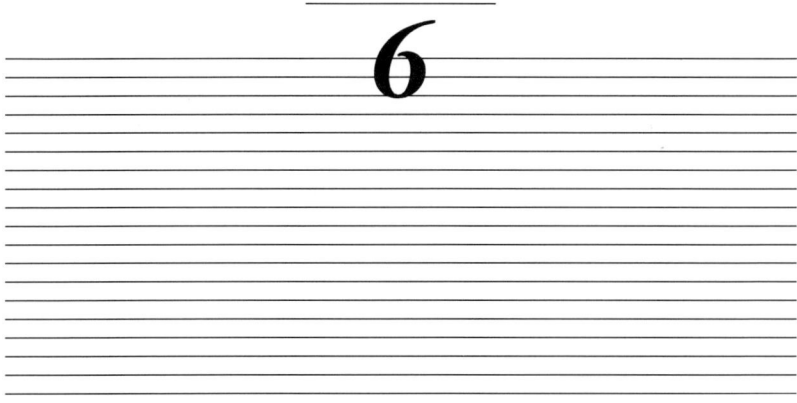

# Dilemmas: Competition and Coordination

Competitive relations among colleges and universities are a natural outgrowth of the means this nation has chosen for protecting the academic freedom and institutional autonomy of the collegiate institution. We have decentralized the control of universities and colleges and created an environment in which the success, and even the survival, of individual institutions depend on their vigor in competing for funds from a variety of sources, including students and their families, private philanthropy, and support of various kinds from local, state, and national governments. Diversification of institutions' sources of funds and seats of control safeguards their independence; the forces of competition also help produce a higher education system whose diversity, energy, and commitment to excellence are the envy of the world.

Yet not all the consequences of competition are good. As we noted earlier, there seems to be a strong tendency for a competitive environment to push schools toward trying to admit the best students they can; typically, the schools that are endowed with the most resources and the best faculty will win that competition. Yet it is by no means obvious, either on equity or efficiency grounds, that this is the most desirable way to allocate higher education resources.

Other aspects of competition, both among schools and among students, may have undesirable consequences as well. This chapter first clarifies the nature of the forces that may tend to produce these undesirable side effects of competition and, second, investigates the difficult question of how we might ameliorate these undesirable side effects without giving up the enormous benefits competition provides for both the effectiveness and the autonomy of higher education.

## Competitive Forces

We begin by investigating more closely the logic of the competitive admission "game" that results in the "best" students converging on the wealthiest institutions. In principle, it would not seem obvious that competitive forces should work this way. Schools differ in their missions, and hence in the clienteles they aim to serve. The resources a school has available to pursue its mission might, to some extent, reflect the urgency society attaches to its pursuit. So, in principle, if society valued the redress of inequality or felt that investments in learning by low-achieving students have a good return, institutions that serve less qualified or less affluent students would have lower student-faculty ratios, more prestigious faculty, and so on. Schools with a clear sense of mission would obviously want to select students who would fit well with the missions they had adopted. Presumably, they would be equally inclined to reject students who were overqualified and those who were underqualified for their programs.

Clearly, this does not happen. Schools that are selective in admission almost always gauge their success by how strong their student body is in terms of conventional measures such as grades and test scores. Any student who was turned down by a school for being "too good" could be assured of a front page headline in the *Chronicle of Higher Education*. Moreover, students are often more interested in getting into the "best" school that will admit them—judging best by the average academic level of students—than by searching for the program that provides the best fit for themselves.

There are several reasons for this. Perhaps the primary reason is interdependence among students in the process of learning, discussed

## Dilemmas: Competition and Coordination

in Chapter 5. Available evidence, and certainly common belief, suggest that typically a student will learn more when exposed to brighter classmates. At least within limits, this provides an obvious motivation for students to seek out schools with high-achieving student bodies. In the same way, an individual institution will typically be able to offer any given student a better education if it can provide that student with high-achieving classmates. These two forces are enough to explain why schools use their resources to compete for the best students, and why strong students seek to be with other strong students.

These learning effects may well be complemented by reputation or halo effects of different kinds. Schools may benefit by taking credit for the high quality of their students. (Harvard President Charles Eliot once explained that his institution had come to be such a great storehouse of knowledge because the freshmen arrived with so much and left with so little.) Below-average students at an institution may similarly hope to be judged by the average quality of the institution's graduates. Notice, however, that, halo effects aside, genuine learning effects may well be enough to justify the efforts of individual institutions and students to associate themselves with the "best and the brightest."

Yet, as the arguments in Chapters 3 and 4 suggest, the private benefits to students and schools from this competition may not be matched by the social benefits. When a school entices a high-quality student from another institution, the gains to students at the "winning" institution will roughly equal the losses to those at the "losing" institution. If the learning effects at the two schools are equivalent, whatever resources go into the competition between schools for this student are wasted from the social viewpoint. If, as may well be the case, there is a negative net effect on learning of moving a strong student from a school with weaker students to a school with stronger students, then competitive efforts in this respect may well be socially counterproductive.

The potential for wasteful or unproductive competition seems substantial. Schools spend considerable resources trying to influence marginal choices of students among schools. From the point of view of any one of these schools, these efforts are absolutely essential. Losing good students would make it harder to attract other good students (and good faculty), and the possibility of a downward spiral would loom. Yet, from a social point of view, it is far from clear that these efforts improve the allocation of good students.

These competitive pressures may also produce even more clearly negative results. One obvious example is that a school's selectivity, and therefore desirability, is often measured by the numbers of students it rejects. This gives institutions an incentive to entice students to apply simply for the purpose of rejecting them. Schools may also enrich their entering classes through the offer of merit-based ("non-need-based") scholarships. When this involves schools with similar educational programs and student body compositions, it is a socially wasteful use of college resources on students who, by definition, do not need the assistance. The opportunity cost of this spending is presumably reduced support either for need-based student aid or for other educational purposes of the institution. (On the other hand, there may be cases in which the offer of non-need-based scholarships at less prestigious institutions, with the aim of attracting top students who would not otherwise consider enrolling there, might have desirable effects on the distribution of students; we return to this point below.)

Farther afield from the topic of admissions, competition for students may also be a force encouraging spending around campuses on various kinds of conspicuous consumption that impress and attract students without adding materially to the educational performance of the institution.[1]

The competitive process may influence students as well as institutions in negative ways. Here again, the effects of this competition are a mixed bag. Perhaps the most important positive effect is the stimulus it gives to students to perform well in high school. For those students who have the aspiration and the resources to attend a selective college, there is an incentive to do well, both in strictly academic pursuits and in those kinds of extracurricular activities that college admission committees consider. On the other hand, these incentives may lead students to efforts that have little point other than improving their chances for college admission. These efforts range from enrolling in special courses aimed at improving SAT scores to signing up for

---

1. McPherson, Schapiro, and Winston (1989a) presented data showing that the richest private colleges increased their capital spending on physical plant by 266 percent in real terms during the period 1978–1986, compared with only 4 percent among the poorly endowed. A similar, but less obvious, pattern is apparent among more and less well-endowed private universities. See McPherson and Winston (1988) for possible explanations.

extracurricular activities simply to "look good on paper." The psychological pressure to do well in the admission "rat race" may also have damaging effects on the development of young people (Wolff, 1969).

## Cooperative Agreements

What are the prospects for curtailing the undesirable side effects of admission competition without undermining the genuinely desirable effects of competition among both schools and students? The most promising avenue for this kind of response may well be through forms of cooperative agreements among schools. Precedent exists: Some groups of selective institutions already have agreements that help regulate competition in student aid awards, through schools' adherence to agreed formulas for awarding need-based student aid and agreements not to award non-need-based scholarships. Much more explicit and thorough agreements exist among schools in common athletic conferences concerning admission and financial aid practices. These agreements often cover numbers of students and recruitment practices as well as amounts of financial aid to be awarded.

We could imagine groups of colleges seeking to develop analogous agreements to govern recruitment practices and admission decisions more generally. To make it concrete (perhaps unrealistically so), picture the Ivy League schools comparing the musical talent among their common applicants and arriving at an agreement that would ensure a good orchestra at every school. Such agreements could be highly explicit (as are athletic admission agreements), even to the point of dictating, say, how many students with SAT scores above 1350 a school would accept. They could also be more informal and limited: Schools could, for example, agree to refrain from certain recruiting practices (such as paying for visits to campus for highly desirable students) or could agree to pool some marketing efforts for the sake both of efficiency and of promoting more accurate and informative advertising.

It is useful to distinguish between two possibilities, which might be termed inequality-preserving and inequality-reducing agreements. Schools obviously differ enormously in the advantages they currently enjoy in recruiting. One class of agreements would be those that avoided challenging the admission "pecking order" that currently exists, in effect aiming to maintain something like the existing distribution of students among schools, but with less effort and waste. A second class would really attempt to change the rules in ways that redistributed talent significantly, presumably with the effect of reducing the amount of sorting that goes on in the admission process.

## *Inequality-Preserving Agreements*

It is much easier to imagine schools settling on inequality-preserving agreements. Thresher (1966) pointed out that there has been a fair amount of cooperation among institutions of higher learning in the United States in terms of the evaluation of financial need, the development of standardized tests, etc. However, he stated:

> large groups of colleges have been able, in the pursuit of their own individual ends, to agree on these measures only because these measures are designed to run parallel to the interests of each, and so are to a large extent noncontroversial. Cooperative agencies among colleges tend to include activities in which the interests of the members run parallel. The really difficult problems at Level Three concern differential interests among colleges, the areas of conflict and competition in which the ostensible or supposed interest of the college runs counter to the public interest, or to that of individual students, or to that of other colleges. (p. 67)

Existing athletic conferences are more or less of this inequality-preserving/parallel-interest character: Conferences tend to group schools of similar athletic aspirations, and the rules tend to ensure that schools that have traditionally had exceptionally strong athletic programs will preserve that advantage. Similarly, agreements within a limited group of schools to resist offering non-need-based awards make it harder for less prestigious schools within the group to attract the best students, thus tending to preserve the pecking order among schools that are party to the agreement. (This obviously creates an incentive for less prestigious schools to withdraw from the group. Against this is the consideration that schools may derive other important benefits from continued membership.) Thus, it is not difficult to imagine a group of strong New England institutions entering into agreements that would govern aspects of the admission competition among them. As long as these schools jointly preserved the same pool of admitted students they have now, restraining the competition among themselves in attracting those students might be seen by these schools as being in their interest.

A fresh illustration of this kind of cooperation was reported in the *Chronicle of Higher Education* for October 4, 1989. A group of 44 colleges and universities entered an agreement not to publicize the average SAT scores of their entering classes. Presumably, one effect of such an agreement, and part of its purpose, is to reduce the emphasis these schools may place on strong SAT scores in the entering class as a recruiting device for other students. A less happy, and possibly unintended, consequence is that the suppression of information about average SAT scores may encourage applications from some students who are unlikely to be admitted. Students may also be deprived of information about the quality of their potential classmates that would help them to make a good choice among colleges. If these negative effects are not too serious, this kind of cooperation might be a small step toward deescalating admission competition among a group of schools without much affecting the ultimate destination of students who apply to more than one of the group.

## *Inequality-Reducing Agreements*

It is much harder to imagine the Ivies, for example, arriving at an agreement that would result in some of their stronger candidates for admission being diverted to a set of less prestigious institutions. Such inequality-reducing agreements might be desirable from the point of view of the public interest if, in fact, a wider distribution of the most able students had educational advantages. The problem is that in negotiations over this kind of agreement there would be clear winners and losers among the schools that participated. Second-tier universities would obviously be eager to enter an agreement to distribute top-ranked students more widely; it is much less likely that first-tier institutions would see any benefit in doing so. Such an agreement would be analogous to National Collegiate Athletic Association (NCAA) Division I football schools agreeing to limit the number of top-ranking football prospects they recruited in order to be sure there were some nationally ranked players available to Division II schools. Whether such an agreement would be socially productive is beyond our ability to judge; that Division I would resist it is undisputed.

## Results of Cooperative Agreements

Even inequality-preserving agreements among a group of schools may have desirable side effects on the overall distribution of students. Consider the earlier example of agreements not to award non-need-based scholarships. Notice that such agreements actually make it easier for nonparticipants to compete. A less prestigious school, for example, can "bid" students away from the Ivies without much concern about counterbids, precisely because the Ivies adhere to an agreement among themselves not to make non-need-based awards. Attracting a few academic "stars" to an institution where they are relatively scarce may have important benefits for the learning of other students at the institution, and may also make it easier for the school to attract higher-quality faculty. If, as discussed in Chapter 5, there are net benefits to mixing students of different abilities, the benefits at the receiving school can be expected to outweigh the loss to students who remain at the institution from which the superior students were drawn. Notice, however, that the students who relocate in response to the award offer are likely to incur some costs. If the human capital model of education is correct, this loss may result from a diminished amount of learning at a lower-quality institution; alternatively, if the credentialing model holds, the loss may result from the perception that any student attending a school that is less prestigious (based on the average quality of students) is also less qualified. The non-need-based award to a student making this choice might well be viewed as a reasonable compensation for the costs involved.[2]

Thus voluntary cooperative agreements among colleges to regulate recruiting and admission practices might help to rein in competitive excess, and even have some favorable effects on the distribution of students. However, given the unlikelihood that schools will agree to policies that conflict substantially with their individual interests, voluntary agreements will surely not be a route to any fundamental change in admission practices, even if such changes are seen as desirable. Still, the potential benefits of these more limited agreements

---

2. To put this in economic terms, efforts to lower the net price through non-need-based scholarships may offset lower returns due to attending a less prestigious institution (whether these lower returns are due to human capital or credentialing effects). Hence, the rate of return may be the same as that obtained at a more prestigious (but more costly) institution.

could be significant. Imagine, for example, that groups of schools competing for similar groups of students agreed to distribute information about their schools—such as admission brochures—in a single common format, perhaps packaging the information in a joint booklet. They might similarly limit and coordinate postadmission recruiting efforts—such as yield parties (held to entice students to enroll once admitted). Done sensibly, such agreements might reduce recruiting costs to schools while actually increasing the flow of useful information (and reducing the amount of hype) disseminated to students.

## *Coordination of Admission Policies*

The more ambitious step of explicit coordination, whether of recruiting practices or general admission policies, might raise significant questions. Would such policies be fair to individual students, some of whom might benefit from unbridled competition? Would agreements to coordinate policies tend to undermine the kind of active competition among schools that is an underpinning of educational excellence and autonomy? Would such agreements run afoul of antitrust laws? (This is a question that might appear more pertinent today than in earlier years.)

These questions can really be answered thoroughly only when fully articulated proposals for cooperation are spelled out. Indeed, such existing cooperative practices as "overlap" meetings, at which colleges compare notes on their judgment of the ability of individual families to pay for education, are seen by some to raise these issues. As a general matter, however, it would seem that a wide range of cooperative policies could meet the tests implied by the questions raised above. Some policies presumably would not pass muster: If schools, for example, agreed to set a quota on the number of students they would accept with SAT scores above a certain cutoff, those excluded by such a policy could rightly object that their credentials had been denied equal consideration with those of less qualified students who were admitted. But if policies do not deprive applicants of the opportunity for equal consideration, there seems to be no obvious ground for asserting that particular students deserve to get as good a "deal" as they might expect to get under unbridled competition. Students, for example, might claim to be harmed by a policy against non-need-based scholarships, compared with a competitive situation in which they would qualify for such an award. But if the agreement to prohibit non-need-based awards serves purposes that are socially valuable and reasonably related to the goals of the colleges that subscribe to it, there seems to be no validity to the claim that a student has a right to the benefits he or she would get if a different policy were in effect. Similarly, as long as agreements among schools serve the schools' educational missions and further the public interest, only an irrational attachment to competition for its own sake could explain the application of antitrust laws to those agreements.[3] Cooperative agreements may thus serve a useful, if limited, role in improving the existing admission system. Such agreements are among the policy alternatives to be discussed in Chapter 7.

---

3. The U.S. Supreme Court has recognized that many aspects of the agreements that regulate athletic competition among schools—including agreements not to pay players and to regulate recruiting practices—are defensible on these grounds. See *NCAA v. Board of Regents of the University of Oklahoma et al.*, 468 US 85 (June 27, 1984).

# Policies: Big versus Small Changes

The evidence in the preceding chapters leads us to believe that a purely competitive allocation scheme may have some undesirable social consequences. It is clear that the existing system leads to rather sharp stratification of the college-going population by measured ability (and hence, by family background). Further, vastly different amounts of resources are devoted to the education of different groups of students, with low-income and educationally disadvantaged students getting the short end of the stick.

These arrangements seem inequitable on their face and, although the evidence is somewhat ambiguous, may be educationally inefficient as well. Does our analysis suggest changes that may improve the current system in terms of social outcomes? If so, are relatively minor changes sufficient or is more radical action called for? In this chapter, we examine the range of possibilities, beginning with the most extreme.

# A Radical Alternative: Pure Open Admission

Perhaps the most radical alternative to the current system would be an enforced requirement of open admission at all institutions.[1] To make this proposal more than a slogan, we must be specific about what it means. Open admission must be open to all students who are above some threshold, which might be possession of a high school diploma, or simply a declaration by some appropriate body that a student has the "ability to benefit" from further study. The full impact of open admission is felt if we assume that the threshold is set low, and that it is the same at all institutions. Moreover, open admission might usefully be assumed to imply making institutions open financially, as well as academically, to all comers. Thus, in considering the implications of this radical alternative, we should assume that funds are somehow available either to make tuition quite low everywhere or (somewhat less implausibly) to finance the "demonstrated financial need" of all students. We must also recognize that enforced open admission would be likely to present some institutions with an enrollment demand far exceeding their capacity. Rather than supposing that these institutions would be required to expand to admit all applying students, it seems more reasonable to suppose that these institutions would be allowed to choose among applicants through a random process: Generalized open admission must really mean random admission.[2]

Two final definitional points are needed. A sufficiently large and complex institution could reproduce selectivity internally, by having restrictive admission to certain majors, to "honors" colleges, and the like. Meaningful systemwide open admission must entail severe limitations on such internal differentiation. Similarly, schools could achieve many of the effects of selective admission by having extremely high standards for progress from the freshman to the sophomore year. This would defeat the point of the reform, and would add greatly to the costs borne by students, many of whom would invest in college only to "fail" after one year. In our view, open admission should be assumed to imply standards that permit any reasonably diligent student to remain in good standing at the institution of his or her choice.

---

1. This proposal is examined in Wolff (1969).
2. For a wide-ranging and illuminating discussion of randomization in social decisions, see Elster (1989).

*Policies: Big versus Small Changes*

## *Advantages*

There are several advantages of such a drastic change, including:

**1.** If schools are deprived of the opportunity to select among students, they essentially lose the incentive to recruit more than the number of students needed to fill their classes.[3] If, as suggested above, intense competition for the most able students has driven some schools to excessive investment in such competition-driven amenities as luxurious dormitories and expensive recreational facilities, open admission would tend to discourage such investment.

**2.** As Thresher (1966) noted, open admission would make schools prove their worth; they could not rely on the strong reputation of their students as evidence of their quality.

**3.** It is quite possible, as some of the evidence reviewed earlier suggests, that the mixing of students of different cognitive abilities would produce more benefits than costs. It seems likely that a moderate movement in this direction, away from the current highly stratified system, might have such net benefits; it is not nearly so clear that movement all the way to complete equality would have the consequence of maximizing learning effects.

**4.** Compared with the current mix of credentialism (or screening) and human capital in the existing higher education system, this change would inevitably tilt the system further toward investment in human capital; schools that could not choose among their applicants, and that were highly restricted in their internal differentiation, could contribute relatively little to screening efforts.

**5.** The abolition of the admission "rat race" would dramatically change the pressures on high school students. They would have no reason to spend time and energy trying to inflate their SAT scores artificially, and they would be discouraged from engaging in résumé-enhancing activities that they were not really interested in.

---

3. This is true, at any rate, if the schools cannot find ways to appeal differentially to more able and attractive students. Notice that if schools are compelled to select randomly from among all applicants, it will be much harder for them to make selective appeals on the basis of the character of their student bodies. Moreover, if less able students benefit from being educated with more able students, the very fact that a school succeeds in enriching its applicant pool will tend to attract applications from less able students, tending to offset the enrichment.

## *Disadvantages*

A radical change to open admission would have obvious drawbacks as well:

1. Open admission would require a deep intrusion into the autonomy of higher education institutions, particularly in regard to the regulation needed to discourage the internal differentiation that might otherwise replace selectivity.

2. Open (random) admission would greatly reduce the incentives of institutions to compete for students. Unless institutions could find effective ways to appeal selectively to more able or attractive applicants, there would be no reason for institutions to desire a larger applicant pool than the minimum that would fill the institution. We noted above that the current system may lead to some unproductive forms of competition. However, to the degree that competition encourages institutions to strive to improve their programs, its loss would be undesirable.

3. Although open admission would free high school students from the need for inappropriate efforts to get into better schools, it would also deprive them of the positive incentive effects of selective admission. One of the main reasons to study hard in high school—that of getting into a good college—would be lost.

4. If colleges continued to differ greatly in the quality of their programs, or in the amount of resources they spent per student, distributing these inequalities randomly would seem unfair. If society believes that students who have achieved more by the end of high school "deserve" more or better education, it will be unwilling to accept random distribution of educational opportunity in college.

5. Finally, as noted earlier, complete randomization may well go beyond the ideal amount of mixing of students from the standpoint of promoting efficient learning. Even if it is true (remember that the evidence is far from conclusive) that, at the margin and starting from present levels of inequality, more streaming of students of differing ability would promote learning on balance, it is quite possible that complete equalization would be counterproductive. Intuitively, it seems reasonable that combining students who are extremely different in knowledge and capacity in the same educational program may well impede the performance of both groups.

# Intermediate Proposals: Modified Open Admission

Let us turn from this extreme proposal to arrangements that would fall between pure open admission and the present system of selective admission. Thus we could imagine raising the "floor" of the open admission system from the quite low base just discussed to some higher level. Since there already are a number of institutions, including many community colleges, that already practice open admission, the idea of raising the floor requires us to consider the prospect of having different floors at different groups of institutions. Thus, we might imagine—following a suggestion of Wolff (1969)—the possibility of elite colleges and universities in the Northeast either agreeing on or being compelled to adopt an admission floor that would be quite demanding, but that would still classify as admissible many more applicants than these schools now admit. These schools would then admit students randomly from among the admissible applicants. Other groups of schools might have floors at different levels.

Plainly, if schools set their floors high enough, and if floors varied enough among schools, we could in effect come quite close to reproducing the existing system. However, it seems clear that modified arrangements are possible that would preserve significant elements of the selectivity present in the existing system, while introducing some of the advantages of pure open admission.[4] [Thresher (1966) seemed to have something of this kind in mind in his random admission proposal.] How would such modified arrangements change the assessment of the costs and benefits of pure open admission?

**Institutional autonomy.** Government enforcement of such a system would raise many of the same issues about institutional autonomy that fully random admission raises, although presumably the introduction of some differentiation among schools would lessen the need for regulation of practices that result in differential education within institutions.

However, it is possible, as Wolff (1969) suggests, that a scheme with some of these elements could be developed through voluntary agreements among groups of colleges. We have discussed factors

---

4. Unlike pure open admission, these modified arrangements do not assume any radical equalization of financial opportunity.

bearing on the feasibility of such agreements in Chapter 6. To the degree that such a scheme was arrived at by voluntary agreements among groups of colleges, it would raise far fewer questions about institutional autonomy.

**Incentives for students.** The impact on students would vary with the degree of differentiation among the "floors" of different institutions. Presumably the hurdles facing students who wanted to become admissible to a particular group of schools would be relatively clear and objective. Such a system could, then, retain substantial incentives for students to perform conscientiously in high school—and, unfortunately, also preserve the incentive for many students to get coaching for the SAT and to struggle to improve their paper credentials in other unproductive ways. Probably the biggest impact would be on the best students at strong high schools, who could be relatively sure of admissibility to top-ranked colleges. They would be under less pressure to hone their qualifications to the maximum. This might in some respects reduce the excellence of their preparation, but the relief of pressure would doubtless bring some educational benefits as well.[5]

**Incentives for institutions.** Again, the incentive effects depend on how high and how different admission floors among groups of institutions were. A group of institutions with a high floor would need to make sure they had, collectively and at each institution in the group, enough applicants to fill their classes, presumably with a comfortable cushion of room to spare. Beyond this, excess applicants would be of little consequence. However, if the floor under a group of elite New England institutions were fairly high, the institutions might be pressed to compete quite vigorously to be sure they had enough qualified students to fill their classes. As we have been arguing, these competitive pressures would have both good and bad consequences for education and efficient resource use.

**Distribution of students across institutions.** Obviously, this kind of modified arrangement would preserve much of the stratification of students by measured achievement that presently exists. If the groups of schools that agreed on a common floor were sufficiently broad,

---

5. Wolff (1969) imagines, somewhat flamboyantly, "the nationwide sigh of relief that would go up from hundreds of thousands of anxious, overworked, parent-hounded boys and girls," should such a system be instituted in the Ivy League (p. 144).

some significant mixing of students across ability levels might be encouraged. Moreover, some very strong students would be rejected from a given group of schools at random, and they would enrich the student body composition at other groups of schools. Given the assumption that full randomization is not the optimal arrangement, this sort of development might be quite desirable educationally. However, it seems unlikely that schools would voluntarily join in agreements to share students with schools that were substantially less selective than themselves. Thus, if these arrangements were to be the result of voluntary agreements, they would probably fall into the class of inequality-preserving agreements we discussed in Chapter 6.

# Incremental Changes in the Existing System

The changes considered above fundamentally alter our current admission system in higher education. An alternative would be to make a number of rather modest reforms that, while retaining the basic nature of what is already in place, can move us at least some distance toward both greater equity and increased efficiency.

## *Cooperative Agreements among Institutions*

One such reform would be to foster greater cooperation among institutions in their recruiting efforts. As mentioned in Chapter 6, the distribution of information could be made more cost-effective by limiting "attention-grabbing," public relations–driven brochures and sticking to a common format in describing what each institution has to offer.

Cooperation about limiting expenditures on competition-driven amenities is obviously much more difficult to maintain but, given changes over time in the composition of expenditures (as described above), any effort in this direction should be applauded. One reason that this issue is so difficult to deal with is that the distinction between a "frill" and a valid educational expenditure is subjective; an elaborate new dorm, gym, or classroom building contains elements of both. However, schools in the same athletic conference might have some limits on new facilities; schools with comparable library resources might emphasize sharing over new acquisitions; schools might split the cost of the latest scientific equipment rather than seeking a competitive edge by outbidding other schools.[6] Although these items are not directly related to admission, competition in spending on them is often the indirect result of admission pressures.

Another aspect of cooperation that could be expanded is in the determination of financial aid. An important achievement of the existing student aid system is to base the award of most financial aid on an agreed-upon methodology for determining a family's ability to pay. Moreover, the exchange of information and the sharing of expertise undoubtedly lead to a fairer determination of parental contributions among the many institutions that are currently involved in some form of "overlap" agreement.[7] The number of schools engaged in such a practice can be increased. In addition, the scope of the agreement can be expanded. Currently, schools attempt to coordinate their decisions about total amounts of parental contribution, but then compete vigorously on the particulars of the financial aid package (loan versus grant versus work-study). Schools with very similar clienteles and educational programs find themselves offering what amounts to merit scholarships within the framework of need-based aid. Although we may argue the virtue of offering this type of aid to induce a student to attend a very different type of school, aid offers that simply bid down the price to favored students, without influencing their decision to choose a particular kind of education, are pointless from the viewpoint of society. Therefore, it would be desirable to extend these overlap agreements to include discussion of the components of the package. Current efforts by the Department of Justice and some of the media to imply that cooperative financial aid agreements somehow serve to undermine the public good are obviously at variance with our recommendations to expand such agreements. There is a real danger, in our view, that simple protestations about the evils of coordinated action may move our system in a way that makes it less fair and less efficient.

---

6. The problem of wasting resources is compounded when duplicated facilities are underutilized.

7. Overlap refers to the practice among some groups of schools of comparing the record of any student admitted to more than one of the schools that subscribe to the agreement. The schools involved attempt to reach agreement on the amount the family can contribute to the student's educational expenses.

## *Reallocation of Students*

In addition to these issues of cooperative behavior among schools, there may also be fairly modest reforms that could aid in reallocating students and resources among schools in ways that promote efficiency and equity. As we have noted throughout, there may be educational and social benefits to reducing the degree of stratification of students in higher education. Encouraging some highly able students to attend institutions where the average student is less able may well make important contributions to the learning of the less capable students. The pure open admission discussed above would do this in a dramatic way; merit awards can also sometimes work in this desirable direction.

If elite colleges that enroll the great majority of highly able students refrain from offering merit awards, then other schools may have the opportunity to attract some of these academic stars by offering them attractive financial aid packages. As noted in Chapter 6, by choosing to enroll at an institution offering such an award, the student may pay a price in terms of learning and ultimate financial gain from education. This student is, however, providing educational benefits to his or her classmates—benefits that are probably greater than those that the same student would provide to others at an elite school. The fact that this student's education is obtained at a lower cost may be seen as appropriate compensation for the benefits to others and tends to offset the possible lower educational returns to the individual student. The advantage of this way of redistributing students, compared to the more Draconian schemes discussed earlier, is that the student relocates voluntarily.

Affirmative-action programs also offer a mechanism for modifying the workings of selective-admission policies. Affirmative action means different things to different people. At a minimum, it describes efforts to expand the pool of applicants from historically disadvantaged groups, and to purge selection processes of unintended biases. But it may also mean that members of these groups benefit from some form of preferential admission. In the latter form, affirmative action may promote a degree of streaming of more and less highly qualified students, similar to the programs for redistributing students discussed above. Of course, streaming can be increased either by encouraging stronger students to attend schools where, on average, students are relatively less qualified (as merit scholarships may do), or by enabling relatively less qualified students (some of whom have considerable talents but have lacked the resources to realize them) to attend schools where students, on average, have stronger qualifications (as preferential admission may do). Assuming that preferential admission in the form of affirmative action selects students with strong potential who have had little opportunity to develop their capacities during the course of their primary and secondary education, such a program has obvious equity benefits, and should also produce educational gains for the minority students. The increased diversity of the student body of a school practicing preferential admission may also have educational benefits for the student body at large.

Still, preferential admission for minority students at selective institutions may have drawbacks, from both an equity and an efficiency point of view, that should not be ignored. Drawing off some of the more able minority students from schools they would otherwise attend may well have adverse educational effects on the students who remain at these schools. At the same time, minority students who are admitted to more selective institutions because of preferential admission may find the environment they encounter there unsupportive, or may find that the gap between their academic preparation and that of their more privileged peers is difficult to bridge successfully. These experiences may attenuate or even reverse the benefits that could otherwise be expected to accrue to enrollment at an institution with students with strong academic qualifications. What Thresher (1966) styles level three thinking can change our outlook in instructive ways. The success of any particular selective institution in attracting more minority students is a worthwhile achievement for that institution, but it may come at the expense of other institutions, by attracting minority students who would otherwise attend those institutions.[8]

These are complicated questions on which we wish to avoid making simple pronouncements. But schools that engage in preferential admission have an obligation to follow through with curricular and other policies to help ensure that the potential educational benefits of preferential admission are realized in fact. It is also worth noting—as advocates of affirmative action would surely acknowledge—that these programs are not aimed at redressing broader pat-

---

8. To the extent that affirmative action programs attract more minority students into higher education as a whole, this "zero sum" analysis does not apply.

terns of inequity in the distribution of access to college, such as might be addressed by pure open admission and even (in a more limited way) by the merit scholarship mechanism we have described.

## *Reallocation of Resources*

The reforms discussed so far involve the redistribution of students among schools. A different type of reform would involve redistributing resources among more and less selective schools. We noted in Chapter 2 that the differences in resources per students between highly endowed (and generally more selective) institutions, on the one hand, and poorly endowed (and generally unselective) institutions, on the other hand, are very large. These large disparities may raise questions about both efficiency and equity. It is intuitively plausible that very large differences in expenditures per student (on the order of 13 to 1 between highly endowed private universities and public community colleges) are subject to diminishing returns, and that transferring resources toward less affluent schools would raise total average productivity. (This seems reasonable, at any rate, in regard to value added per student; it is much less clear that redistributing resources that support research would have comparable productivity-improving effects.) We should note, however, that in contrast to the issue of redistributing students among institutions, where there is at least some scattered evidence about the educational effects, we know of no studies that use empirical evidence to predict the effects on educational outcomes of redistributing resources among schools.

Even if there were widespread agreement that this kind of redistribution would be desirable, the highly varied sources of funding for American higher education institutions, and the importance of respecting institutional autonomy, ensure that there is no easy mechanism for accomplishing such redistribution. Still, significant amounts of resources are provided to colleges and universities by the federal government, and the provision of still further resources is encouraged by the tax deductibility of charitable giving to colleges. It would clearly be possible to shape federal policies in ways that would tend to reduce the disparities in resource levels between more and less selective institutions. To some extent, existing federal student aid programs, which tend to support institutions in proportion to their enrollment of needy students, have this effect already. Other programs, such as those for aid to developing institutions and support for historically black colleges, have had a more direct purpose of strengthening institutions that enroll less advantaged students. It would not be difficult to imagine further steps the federal government could take to redistribute its aid toward less elite institutions and those that enroll needier students.

There may be significant links between policies to redistribute resources and those to redistribute students. On the one hand, programs that encourage some high-achieving students to attend institutions where average student achievement levels are lower would certainly be easier to mount if resource disparities among schools were smaller. On the other hand, it is plain that redistributing resources away from the most selective institutions would compound the costs to these institutions of encouraging some of their high-achieving students to enroll elsewhere. The obvious losers in programs that would strengthen less affluent and less selective institutions would be the students in the most affluent and most selective institutions. The equity of such a change seems (at least to us) fairly clear: The students at the most selective institutions are already the beneficiaries of multiple advantages, and it seems reasonable that they should bear some costs in promoting a more equitable society. Yet, such changes may also have educational costs, and, as mentioned above, we know very little about the net educational effects of such redistributive changes. Compensatory programs that target resources toward less advantaged institutions or students might also have the unintended effect of rewarding mediocrity or penalizing excellence. Ideally, extra resources should be aimed toward institutions that contribute high value added despite relatively meager resources. Given the difficulties of measuring value added, however, the tendency may be to target only the meagerness of resources, and at least in some cases the meager resources may be the product of poor performance.

## Conclusions

This review of policies leads us to the following tentative conclusions: Radical change in existing practices of selective admission seems neither feasible nor desirable. In addition to the fact that the direct educational consequences of such policies are uncertain, strong interference with colleges' admission policies, which would be required by radical change, would violate important values of institutional autonomy.

On the other hand, the suggestions described as "modified open admission" cannot be dismissed so easily. To review, one plan calls for different admission floors at different groups of institutions (elite colleges and universities would agree on an admission floor that would be quite demanding but would classify as admissible many more applicants than these schools now admit), with schools admitting students randomly from the list of acceptable applicants. This would preserve significant elements of the selectivity present in the existing system, while introducing significant elements of the randomness or openness that characterize pure open admission.

As discussed above, this proposal has a number of significant benefits, and some potential costs. Although further consideration seems warranted, several issues should be kept in mind when analyzing such a plan.

First, the randomness of the selection process could easily lead to underrepresentation of certain socioeconomic, demographic, or talent groups, particularly for schools with relatively small student bodies. For some factors, such as racial and ethnic diversity, an effort should be made to ensure that the composition of students enrolling in each institution, within a group of schools with the same admission floor, reflects the composition of the total pool of admissible students. For other factors, there may be reason to ensure an appropriate mix of talents; we would not, for example, want all the musically inclined students at a particular school to be tuba players, with no violinists. We regard these, however, as minimal exceptions to a policy that would maintain a strong commitment to randomizing admission and distribution of students.

In addition, student preferences should be given considerable weight in allocating students among schools within the group. A student who meets the admission standard of the group should be permitted to rank the schools in terms of preference, and an effort should be made to satisfy the student's wishes. Thus, among schools where there is excess demand for admission among admissible applicants, successful candidates would be chosen at random; for schools with relatively less demand, student preferences would play a larger role.

Finally, it should be pointed out that great care should be taken

## Selective Admission and the Public Interest

in determining the pool of admissible candidates. Rather than a mechanical test score criterion, a desirable scheme would employ a set of standards much like those currently used by admission officers at individual institutions—standards that leave room for judgment and experience.

A possibly troubling feature of this policy is that some students who would obviously be admitted to a top-flight institution under the existing system of selective admission would now be rejected at random. From the viewpoint of society, this cost might well be judged worth paying for the sake of the various benefits derived from such a change in admission procedures.

For those who consider that problems with our current selective-admission system are not severe enough to warrant such ambitious changes in the way in which the system operates, there may be considerable merit in the various incremental reforms we have discussed.

First, it would be desirable to encourage institutions to reform and limit their own admission and recruitment practices—through the development of more cooperative behavior that would restrain both competition-driven expenditures that add little to educational production and competitive marketing practices that may be misleading or wasteful. We include agreements about the components of the financial aid package as an important example of cooperative behavior. Such agreements can have the desirable effect of minimizing the chances that aid offers simply lower the price for favored students, without changing the kind of institution they choose—thereby, from the viewpoint of society, wasting resources.

Second, affirmative-action programs (including preferential admission), when accompanied by appropriate on-campus efforts to help students succeed, can help encourage the streaming of students of differing social background and measured achievement levels.

Finally, we see real potential benefits in programs that encourage students to redistribute themselves, through the use of merit scholarships and similar incentives, from more selective to less selective institutions. As we have argued, such voluntary movement may provide significant educational benefits to typical students at the less selective institutions involved. Although there may be educational (and eventually economic) costs for the students who choose to move, the provision of a scholarship will tend to offset those costs.

In sum, it is our feeling that the current system of selective admission can be improved in both its equity and efficiency. There are a number of relatively small changes that would allow the current system to do a better job in promoting the public interest, as well as some more substantial ones that should be examined in greater detail.

It is important to note that for the kinds of reforms we have discussed to work, institutions would need to engage in them in the right spirit. Certainly if institutions undertook to change the mix of students they admitted, faculty and administrators would have to be willing to modify their curricula and teaching techniques to get the most from the group of students being enrolled. Similarly, if institutions entered into cooperative agreements concerning student recruiting or limitations on competition-driven amenities, the good will of the institutions would be required because such agreements could never be enforced to the letter.

The ideas in this monograph certainly do not add up to a well-defined plan for reforming admission in higher education, but we hope they have identified significant areas in which further discussion might proceed. Thresher (1966) pointed out the importance of looking at the admission process in U.S. higher education from a distinct viewpoint—that of the system, rather than its component parts. We agree that level three analysis provides a perspective that contributes insights into the failings of the current system and suggests ways in which it can be improved.

# References

Adelman, Clifford. 1986. "To Imagine an Adverb: Concluding Notes to Adversaries and Enthusiasts." In *Assessment in American Higher Education: Issues and Contexts,* edited by Clifford Adelman. Washington, D.C.: Office of Educational Research and Improvement, U.S. Department of Education: 73–82.

Astin, Alexander W., Kenneth C. Green, William S. Korn, Marilynn Schalit, and Ellyne R. Berz. 1988. *The American Freshman: National Norms for Fall 1988.* Los Angeles: The Higher Education Research Institute, Graduate School of Education, University of California, Los Angeles.

Bowles, Samuel, and Herbert Gintis. 1976. *Schooling in Capitalist America.* New York: Basic Books.

Boyer, Ernest L. 1987. *College: The Undergraduate Experience in America.* The Carnegie Foundation for the Advancement of Teaching. New York: Harper & Row.

Chandler, John W. 1986. "Assessment: A View From the Campus." Paper presented at the ETS Invitational Conference, "Assessing the Outcomes of Higher Education," New York City, October.

Coleman, James S., et al. 1966. *Equality of Educational Opportunity.* Washington, D.C.: U.S. Government Printing Office.

College Board. 1988. *Annual Survey of Colleges, 1988-89: Summary Statistics.* New York: College Entrance Examination Board.

# References

Daniere, Andre, and Jerry Mechling. 1970. "Direct Marginal Productivity of College Education in Relation to College Aptitude of Students and Production Costs of Institutions." *The Journal of Human Resources* Winter: 51–70.

Elster, Jon. 1989. *Solomonic Judgments.* New York: Cambridge University Press.

Ewell, Peter T. 1983. *Student-Outcomes Questionnaires: An Implementation Handbook.* 2nd edition. Boulder, Col.: National Center for Higher Education Management Systems.

Gauthier, David. 1986. *Morals by Agreement.* Oxford: Clarendon Press.

Griliches, Zvi, and William Mason. 1972. "Education, Income and Ability." *Journal of Political Economy* May/June, Part II: S74–S103.

Hacker, Andrew. 1989. "Affirmative Action: The New Look." *The New York Review of Books* October 12: 63–68.

Hansen, W. Lee, and Jacob A. Stampen. 1987. "Economics and Financing of Higher Education: The Tension between Equity and Quality." Unpublished.

Hansen, W. Lee, Burton Weisbrod, and William J. Scanlon. 1970. "Schooling and Earnings of Low Achievers." *American Economic Review* June: 409–418.

Hanushek, Eric A. 1973. "Regional Differences in the Structure of Earnings." *Review of Economics and Statistics* May: 204–213.

Hanushek, Eric A. 1978. "Ethnic Income Variations: Magnitudes and Explanations." In *American Ethnic Groups,* edited by Thomas Sowell. Washington, D.C.: Urban Institute: 139–156.

Harris, John. 1972. "Baccalaureate Requirements: Attainments or Exposures?" *The Educational Record* Winter: 59–65.

Harris, John. 1986. "Assessing Outcomes in Higher Education." In *Assessment in American Higher Education: Issues and Contexts,* edited by Clifford Adelman. Washington, D.C.: Office of Educational Research and Improvement, U.S. Department of Education: 13–31.

Hauptman, Arthur, and Maureen McLaughlin. 1988. "Is the Goal of Access to Postsecondary Education Being Met?" Unpublished, 1988.

Hause, John C. 1972. "Earnings Profile: Ability and Schooling." *Journal of Political Economy* May/June, Part II: S108–S138.

Henderson, Vernon, Peter Meiszkowski, and Yvon Sauvageau. 1978. "Peer Group Effects and Educational Production Functions." *Journal of Public Economics:* 97–106.

Karabel, Jerome. 1972. "Perspectives on Open Admissions." *Educational Record* Winter: 30–44.

# References

Lee, John B. 1987. "The Equity of Higher Education Subsidies." June. Unpublished.

McKenna, Barbara. 1983. *Surveying Your Alumni: Guidelines and 22 Sample Questionnaires.* Washington, D.C.: Council for Advancement and Support of Education.

McPherson, Michael S. 1983. "Value Conflicts in American Higher Education: A Survey." *The Journal of Higher Education* May/June: 243–278.

McPherson, Michael S., Morton Owen Schapiro, and Gordon C. Winston. 1988. "The Impact of Government Expenditures on College and University Behavior: An Empirical Study." December.

McPherson, Michael S., Morton Owen Schapiro, and Gordon C. Winston. 1989a. "Recent Trends in U.S. Higher Education Costs and Prices: The Role of Government Funding." *AEA Papers and Proceedings* May: 253–257.

McPherson, Michael S., Morton Owen Schapiro, and Gordon C. Winston. 1989b. "The Impact of Federal Student Aid on Institutions: Toward an Empirical Understanding." In *Studying the Impact of Student Aid on Institutions,* edited by R. H. Fenske. *New Directions for Institutional Research* no. 62. San Francisco: Jossey-Bass, Summer: 31–54.

McPherson, Michael S., and Gordon C. Winston. 1988. "Reflections on Price and Quality in U.S. Higher Education." Unpublished.

National Education Association. 1968. *Ability Grouping.* Research Summary 1968-S3. Washington, D.C.: National Education Association.

Nozick, Robert. 1974. *Anarchy, State, and Utopia.* New York: Basic Books.

O'Neill, Joseph P. 1983. "The Crisis in Integrity." Paper presented at the annual meeting of the American Educational Research Association, Montreal, Canada, April.

Pace, C. Robert, and associates. 1975. *Higher Education Measurement and Evaluation Kit.* Los Angeles: Laboratory for Research on Higher Education, University of California, Los Angeles.

Pace, C. Robert. 1979. *Measuring Outcomes of College.* San Francisco: Jossey-Bass.

Pace, C. Robert. 1983. *College Student Experiences: A Questionnaire.* 2nd edition. Los Angeles: The Higher Education Research Institute, Graduate School of Education, University of California, Los Angeles.

Pace, C. Robert. 1984. *Measuring the Quality of College Student Experiences.* Los Angeles: The Higher Education Research Institute, Graduate School of Education, University of California, Los Angeles.

Rawls, John. 1971. *A Theory of Justice.* Cambridge, Mass.: Belknap Press.

Reder, Melvin W. 1974. "Elitism and Opportunity in U.S. Higher Education."

## References

In *Higher Education and the Labor Market*, edited by M. S. Gordon. New York: McGraw-Hill: 419–426.

Rentz, Robert R. 1979. "Testing and the College Degree." *New Directions for Testing and Measurement.* San Francisco: Jossey-Bass.

Riley, John C. 1979. "Testing the Educational Screening Hypothesis." *Journal of Political Economy* October, Part II: S227–S252.

Schapiro, Morton Owen. 1988. "The Concept of Productivity as Applied to U.S. Higher Education." In *The Concept of Productivity in Institutions of Higher Education.* Quebec: University of Quebec Press: 37–72.

Schultz, T. W. 1971. *Investment in Human Capital.* New York: Free Press.

Schultz, T. W. 1975. "The Value of the Ability to Deal with Disequilibria." *Journal of Economic Literature* September: 827–843.

Spence, A. Michael. 1973. "Job Market Signaling." *Quarterly Journal of Economics* August: 355–374.

Taubman, Paul, and Terence Wales. 1974. *Higher Education and Earnings.* New York: McGraw-Hill.

Thresher, B. Alden. 1966. *College Admissions and the Public Interest.* New York: College Entrance Board.

Thurow, Lester C. 1975. *Generating Inequality: Mechanisms of Distribution in the U.S. Economy.* New York: Basic Books.

Troutt, William E. 1979. "Unbundling Instruction: Opportunity for Community Colleges." *Peabody Journal of Education* July: 253–259.

Vanfossen, Beth E., James D. Jones, and Joan Z. Spade. 1987. "Curriculum Tracking and Status Maintenance." *Sociology of Education* April: 104–122.

Walzer, Michael. 1983. *Spheres of Justice.* New York: Basic Books.

Wang, William K. S. 1975. "The Unbundling of Higher Education." *Duke Law Journal:* 53–90.

Weiss, Andrew. 1983. "A Sorting-cum-Learning Model of Education." *Journal of Political Economy* June: 420–442.

Wigdor, A. K., and W. R. Garner, eds. 1982. *Ability Testing: Uses, Consequences, and Controversies.* 2 vols. Washington, D.C.: National Academy of Sciences.

Wolff, Robert Paul. 1969. *The Ideal of the University.* Boston: Beacon Press.

Wolpin, Kenneth I. 1977. "Education and Screening." *American Economic Review* December: 949–958.